PAGE OF AN EARLY CZECH SERVICE-BOOK.

HUSS AND
HIS FOLLOWERS

By

JAN HERBEN

WITH A FOREWORD

by

REV. G. A. FRANK KNIGHT,

M.A., D.D., F.R.S.E.

Geoffrey Bles   Suffolk St., Pall Mall

London

First published . . *February, 1926*

Made and Printed in Great Britain by Butler & Tanner Ltd., Frome and London

Foreword

IN the Great Square in Prague opposite the Town Hall, in front of which in 1621 twenty-seven Protestant leaders were executed after the Battle of the White Mountain, the visitor to the city notices the enormous and massive Memorial to John Hus. The martyr stands amid a group of Bohemian patriots, calling on them to rise and be free. Some of the figures around him are still asleep, some are awaking, some are in the act of springing up, some are fully erect with outstretched hands welcoming the new era of liberty.

The Monument is a symbol of the Bohemian nation to-day. It has arisen from the enforced sleep of centuries, and those ideals for which Hus strove—love of country, of freedom, of righteousness, of integrity in Church and State—are now in large measure incarnate in the Czech people. When the five-hundredth anniversary of his martyrdom occurred in 1915, waves of intense emotion, religious fervour, and patriotic zeal swept over Bohemia. Subscriptions to rear a monument worthy of their greatest hero flowed in from all parts of the world where Hus' name was held in reverence, while in almost every other town and village in the country statues to him were simultaneously erected. It is one of the most striking tributes ever borne to the enduring value of a noble personality that after 500 years the name of " Mister Jan Hus," as he is always called, should still have such abounding power, and that the nation from which he sprang should feel that in this martyr who died at the stake in 1415 the highest ideals of the Czech peoples were embodied. There is no other parallel case known to history. Other nations have had their famous heroes and honour is paid to them. But in reality Bohemia has but one hero, who stands out pre-eminent above all the others— although they derived their light and inspiration from him—and to-day the utmost reverence is shown by almost all classes to the memory of the greatest man to which the Czech race has given birth. John Hus is living still in the hearts, the lives, the aims, and the aspirations of those millions of Czechs in Europe and across the seas, who realize that in him their loftiest conceptions of duty, patriotism, and spiritual freedom found expression.

Why this is so will be seen by those who read the following graphic narrative by Mr. Herben. It will come as a surprise to many to learn how the spirit of Hus was perpetuated in men like Žižka, Prokop, Komensky and others, and how far flung was the influence of the Constance martyr throughout Europe and even throughout the world. To-day Hus is coming into his own, the more his ideals are studied. His was in many ways a far nobler character than that of Luther. To a very marked degree he was a pioneer, and his stand for truth which he sealed at the stake constitutes an era in the world's spiritual history. Where else can the duty of a Christian man be more magnificently summed up than in the famous saying of Hus as I have seen it affixed to the walls of many a structure, in towns such as Budejovice and elsewhere :

" Seek the Truth, Listen to the Truth, Learn the Truth, Love the Truth, Speak the Truth, Hold the Truth, Defend the Truth, until death " ?

It is remarkable how, when one leader falls, another is raised up to carry on his work, but as a rule on different lines. A Moses, the lawgiver, is followed by a Joshua, the warrior. So when Hus the spiritual preacher, the fearless champion of truth, the saint, died amid the flames, his patriotic task was continued by the sword of the invincible Žižka. The stories of his exploits as he fought in the Wars of the Lord are among the most extraordinary and romantic with which history can furnish us. I have stood beside the stone Communion Table in the Great Square at Tabor —the last survivor of twelve such—and it is thrilling to realize how often, after partaking there of the Sacrament, Žižka and his heroes went forth singing " Ye who are the warriors of God," and how the Papal armies fled before them like sheep. But again, when the period of active fighting was over, God had in reserve another leader endowed with different gifts. Komensky was a powerful preacher, a man of prophetic insight and spiritual force, but he was also an educational reformer of the front rank, one far ahead of his time, a scholar whose genius is only now coming to be fully realized. And it is well that Mr. Herben has linked with these great names that of Masaryk, the beloved President of the Czecho-Slovak Republic, in whose soul there burns the same ardour for personal and religious freedom as his famous predecessors showed, and who has suffered and triumphed with his people in their hour of supreme trial and of supreme victory.

It is, further, most striking to observe how the Cup

has become the symbol of Bohemia's living Church to-day. One of the main things for which Hus had contended was the right of all believing men and women to partake of the Cup in the Sacrament of the Lord's Supper, as against the Romanist practice of retaining it solely for the priests. And no sooner had Hus been burnt at Constance than the Bohemians who favoured his views adopted the Cup as their national symbol. In this capacity it has survived the merciless persecutions of centuries. To-day one sees it everywhere—on the front of all Protestant pulpits, stamped on Bibles, inwoven on banners, inscribed on tombstones, affixed to official documents, worn on the lapels of men's coats and ladies' jackets in the form of a neat badge, adorning the gables of Protestant Churches and houses, giving its name " Kalich " to the leading Church newspaper, and even selected in 1919, after the expulsion of the Hapsburgs and the inauguration of the Republic, as the design for the first printed postage-stamp. Here again is another symbol of the triumph of Hus' ideals after 500 years.

The great break-away from Rome in 1920 whereby nearly two million Czechs quitted the Papal Church in a body, and founded the Czecho-Slovak Church, is still another testimony to the power of Hus' teaching and example. What the priests demanded from the Pope in the twentieth century by way of reforms within the Church was just what Hus had claimed in the fifteenth century. Hus perished for his boldness for the Gospel : Dr. Farsky and his fellow-priests of the Czecho-Slovak Church, though excommunicated, drew after them a vast body of patriots who are now rejoicing in their spiritual freedom. But it was the idealism of Hus which inspired the revolt from Rome which is now sweeping over the Republic, and bringing to the country new spiritual life.

This year another striking proof has been given how Hus' ideas of freedom have imbued the nation. A recent Papal decree prohibited the Sacrament from being given to anyone who was a member of the Social Democratic party. The order was issued in French and German, but not in Czech, and for a time it remained unknown. When its tyrannical character became known, the Czecho-Slovak Government at once retaliated by three striking blows. First, it abolished the old laws which made it so difficult for a Roman Catholic to change his faith. Second, it cancelled the regulation that the 16th June should be maintained as a national holiday in honour of St. John of Nepomuk, the Roman Catholic patron saint of Bohemia, whose very existence modern research has proved to be mythical. And third, it decreed that the 6th July, the date of Hus' birth and of his martyrdom, should for all time to come be celebrated annually as the greatest national festival of the Republic.

Yes : Hus still lives, and will continue to live so long as there are Czechs to love his memory and to practise his undying principles of right and truth. This book will have served a noble purpose if in any degree it makes known the beauty, the pathos, the tragedy, the glory, and the romance of the story of " John Hus and his followers."

G. A. FRANK KNIGHT.

Contents

11

List of Illustrations

I

The Bohemian Nation

A Survey of its Evolution

THE Czech nation is a branch of the Slavonic race. During "the wandering of nations," the Czechs penetrated farthest west of all the Slavs and thus formed an enclave amongst the Germanic peoples. Later, when the Magyars established themselves in their present territories, they isolated the Czechs from the Serbs, Croatians and Slovenes, leaving only the Poles as neighbours.

It was not before the sixth century that the Czech nation appeared on the stage of history. When first observed by both the Western and Byzantine historians, its life was still semi-barbaric. By embracing Christianity in the ninth century, it escaped the fate of the Slavs then living along the Baltic Sea and the River Elbe. Joining then the society of the Western nations, it lived in a manner similar to theirs until the fourteenth century. The settlements scattered among forests and swamps became villages, the nobles built themselves castles ; and, finally, the kings, the nobles and the Church founded, in the thirteenth century, a number of towns, which they peopled almost exclusively with German colonists.

Until the fourteenth century the Czechs had no
history of their own. There is only a history of their
princes and kings ; a history which includes many
wars, a series of palace intrigues not without bloodshed, and also attempts at forming a great Czech State,
at one time in the direction of Poland and then again
across the Danube as far as the Adriatic Sea—all this,
however, was nothing but a passing glory. In their
mode of life our ancestors linked themselves with the
State and Church institutions prevailing in the Western
Christian countries at that time. And it seems,
really, that this adaptation to Western culture was even
more advantageous to the Czech nation than the
initial Byzantine influences of the apostles Cyril and
Methodius, who introduced Christianity. The early
literature of the country reveals in its extant fragments
its international origin, whether Latin, German or
French. But at the same time the Czechs have never
been a " bridge between the West and the East "—
for this is altogether a modern ideal.

According to an ancient tradition, the first Czech
prince, Přemysl, was called to the throne from the
plough. Under the patriarchal rule of the Přemyslides the nation made considerable development.
Inhabiting a basin-like territory surrounded and pro-
tected by mountains, it maintained both its language
and the country's prosperity, although some of the
dangers which it encountered were due to the dynasty
itself. This dynasty was becoming strongly Germanized, and there were occasions when, as an Elector of
the German Empire, it jeopardized the country's
independence. Only after the extinction of the
Přemyslid dynasty in 1305 did a *Czech nation* finally
emerge, that is, a nation with a full consciousness of

its Czech and Slavonic nationality and a typical national character. Of this consciousness the best evidence is provided by Dalemil's chronicle ; and its destructive character is noticeable in the manner in which the Czech nation began to differ from its neighbours. Of course, no examination is any longer capable of revealing the influences which were instrumental in forming our national character, yet certain it is, that towards the end of the Přemyslid era the Czech language was already being adopted by scholars, that it moved from the villages, towns and castles into books, and even began to replace both Latin and German.

It is not surprising that the Czech nation became conscious of its nationality earlier than its neighbours, the Poles and Magyars, for since the time of the Přemyslides, Bohemia has always been disputed by two nations. The Přemyslides were, through their Court, very closely bound up with the German princes ; and these also brought into the country German colonists such as skilled artisans, miners, etc. Thus it came about that the rulers of Bohemia filled the bishop's see in Prague with German prelates, handed over the monasteries to German monks and called German clerks to their offices.

The mutual hatred of two neighbouring nations, even when at war, is mild in comparison with that of two different nations living in the same country and perpetually in conflict over divergent interests, especially if one of them be afforded protection and privilege.

This tension in no way diminished when the Bohemian throne was occupied by the Luxemburg dynasty, 1310–1437. The Czechs elected, after some confusion, the 14-year-old John of Luxemburg, the son of the German Emperor of that time, to be their ruler.

This first Luxemburg of Franco-German descent was an extravagant, adventurous knight who visited Bohemia only when in need of money. A man of warlike character, he extended the borders of the Bohemian realm in several directions, but increased the confusion and disorder inside them to the point of an economic catastrophe. He did not love the country he was called to rule over, and even offered it to Bavaria in exchange for the Palatinate. His heroic death at Crecy is well known. But his son Charles (this name he adopted in France, where he was brought up at the court of King Charles—his baptismal name being in reality Venceslas), who became later the Roman Emperor Charles IV, made himself for ever famous in Bohemia. When he was still co-regent he showed his love for Bohemia, and when he subsequently ascended the throne he devoted himself to the interests of the country, and especially to the national language. He was aware of the fact that the German Imperial throne, to him of great importance, would only rest on a firm foundation if supported by the power and capacity of his own domains.

Great is the number of enterprises by which Charles successfully improved the lands of the Bohemian crown and earned the name of " The Father of his Country." He enhanced the material wealth of the country and enriched the moral and intellectual life of the nation, by introducing a strict administration of justice, and compelling respect for the law. He also considerably increased the territory of the Bohemian State and that almost without using the sword. The two parts of the capital of Bohemia, Prague, spread on both banks of the Vltava, he connected with an expensive bridge and enlarged the town itself by almost a half, with the intention of making it the Paris of Central Europe. He also built stately churches, monasteries and castles. Through his efforts Prague became the junction for all the traffic of Central Europe. The Southern Slavs gave it the name of " Zlatá Praha " (Golden Prague). But above all—and a point of the greatest importance to us—was the fact that Prague became a centre of European civilization when, in 1348, Charles founded there a university, which, by its surprising growth, soon became worthy of its older sisters at Bologna, Paris and Oxford. Here, at the University, the Czechs tried conclusions with their neighbours, whom they soon equalled in ability, eagerness to learn and intellectual development.

The greatest glory was bestowed upon the University by Magister John Huss, both as Rector and as a popular preacher at the Bethlehem Chapel, where sermons were preached in Czech. For, in the time of Charles III and his son Václav (Venceslas), the German language was predominant both in public offices and in the churches and schools all over the country. The efforts made by Huss for a reform of religious life we call the Bohemian Reformation.

A reformation was certainly needed in a Church which had become notorious for its moral corruption, its covetousness and its love of wealth and pleasure. The clergy led a profligate and voluptuous life, thereby giving great offence to the believers. In Bohemia the conditions in this respect were indeed deplorable. The Emperor Charles, by his generous support of the Church and the clergy, had considerably increased both its wealth and splendour, so that there soon arose countless churches and monasteries on all sides and many new benefices and foundations were established ; but neither the Church nor the clergy gained in true devotion and moral nobility. On the contrary, their demoralization and utter abandonment to all kinds of vices became almost universal.

So long as Huss was castigating Church abuses in a general way, he met with sympathy and even praise, but the moment he turned against the immoral life of the priests themselves he was suspected of heresy. And a real heretic, as regards Church history, he became soon afterwards when, following his long theological doubts and disputes, he sought information of the English heretic Wyclif, and thus entered upon the road travelled by all reformers. He found that the Church tenets conflicted with the Gospel, which was to him a source of religious perception. Finally, at the Council of Constance (1415) Huss parted with Rome not merely on account of a few dogmatic articles but also because of the mediæval principle, according to which the Christian must, in matters of faith, submit to papal decrees in all circumstances. Huss did not refuse to submit either to the Pope or to the Council of Constance, but he opposed to the authority of the Church a new principle, that of the personal intellect and personal conviction of the Christian, supported by his conscience. Huss, therefore, declined to retract his real or supposed errors ; he asked to be both taught and convinced by arguments. This was altogether a new idea—for it signified new principles and new rules of life in the mediæval darkness. And herein, too, lies the enormous significance of Huss.

When in 1415 Huss was burnt at the stake in Constance, the whole Czech nation rallied to his views, accepting his principle of personal conviction and his efforts to secure a moral reform of society. The pious among the people began to hold great gatherings in the mountains, to which they gave Biblical names, and in this manner organized themselves into a new religious body. This signified, in regard to the Church and State authorities, nothing but a rebellion, which at last, in 1419, broke out openly in Prague.

The armed forces of the people were led by John Žižka, who turned Bohemia into a fortified camp by creating a new kind of army and inventing a new military organization. Having at his disposal no other material than the peasant class, he organized from their ranks an infantry which fought from within movable wagon bastions against the cavalry, which then still formed the core of both the feudal and State troops. In a few battles, by these so-called " iron blows," he crushed the domestic cavalry, and when the Pope and Emperor Sigmund proclaimed crusades by the whole of Europe against the Bohemian Hussites, Žižka knew how to defend the country against an immense superiority of numbers, and by several bloody defeats drove the Crusaders from Bohemia. The seat of Žižka's military power was at Tábor, a new town ingeniously designed and impregnably fortified by him in south-eastern Bohemia. When Žižka, " the leader unconquered," although already blind in both eyes, died in 1424, two priests were chosen as leaders of the Hussite (Táborite) armies : Prokop the Great and Prokop the Lesser.

The Hussite wars lasted fifteen years. Under Prokop the Great the Bohemian armies undertook retaliatory expeditions into the German countries, penetrating as far as the Danube and the Baltic Sea, spreading abroad the terror of the Hussite name. The proclamations of the Hussite armies show exactly

what, five years after Huss' death, Hussitism stood for.
The armies called themselves " fighters of the Lord,"
i.e., armies fighting for a religious idea, but at the same
time they were also warring for the " Czech tongue,"
that is, for national rights against German usurpation.
The symbol of Hussitism was a chalice, with which
their battle-flags were decorated.   Thus Bohemia became a country of the Gospel and the chalice, or
Calixtines (or Utraquists, as the Holy Communion was
introduced in the form of bread and wine).

At the first Hussite diet at Čáslav in 1421 the representatives of the nation deposed the King and revoked
their obedience to the Pope.   The Hussite wars
having ended so victoriously, Rome began to treat
with the Hussites peaceably, and at the Council of Basel
recognized them as true sons of the Church, granting
the Bohemian national Church four deviations from
the ordinary Catholic confession, even permitting the
Czechs to elect a Hussite archbishop (Rokycan).
This agreement is known as the Compacts.   When
the then Emperor Sigmund, brother of the late King
Václav, also promised to keep these Compacts, the
Czechs received him in grace again.   Hussitism gave
birth to a great number of notable men, excelling in
learning, statesmanship and the art of war.   Despite
the fact that Prague University had been purely
national since 1409, when the Germans left it on
account of Huss' activities, its reputation for learning
did not thereby suffer any loss.   With the awakened
national consciousness common education also grew
and schools flourished.   In the military town of Tábor
there were schools, even for girls, the perfection of
which surprised Aeneas Silvius not a little on his visit
to that town.   After the death of Sigmund's grand-

son, the Czechs elected a king from among the native nobility. Their choice fell upon George of Poděbrad, who, after having been the administrator of the State since 1448, was, in 1458, anointed as a King—our only Hussite King. His reign was a successful one ; prosperity, which after the Hussite wars came to an end, returning to the country under his rule. We Czechs honour him also for his efforts in the cause of peace, for he tried to induce the European rulers to form a league of peace, which should prevent future wars and which, in particular, should not allow Rome to incite one nation against the other. Yet Rome once more soaked the Bohemian lands with blood. The Pope soon repealed the Compacts, refused to acknowledge Rokycan, simply declared the Czech nation and King George to be accursed heretics, and caused the neighbouring nations to launch new crusades against the Czechs. King George resisted victoriously, but he died as early as 1471, first, however, recommending a King of Slavonic race as his successor. Thus the throne of Bohemia was occupied for a time by two Polish Kings of little ability. The second of them (Louis) was drowned in 1526 in the swamps near Mohacs in Hungary while taking part in an expedition against the Turks.

During King George's reign there arose in the Czech nation a new religious body called the *Bohemian Brotherhood*. These Bohemian Brothers represented religion, in the sense in which the Czech people conceived of it themselves : a simple avowal of Christ's teaching, and a moral life after the model of the first apostolic communities. A community of people without a sword, the Brotherhood is the flower of the Czech religious and civic spirit. To it belongs the sixteenth century, in which its famous bishop Blahoslav translated, with his disciples, the Scriptures in a rendering called after the town where it was printed, the " Králická Bible " from the original, and in a language so beautiful that it became and has remained the standard of our tongue to this day. Altogether, the " Brothers " greatly enriched Czech literature and raised the standard of both school education and art to a high degree; the " Brothers' Cantionale " (hymn-book) is a forecast of the later musical development among the Czechs.

The fifteenth and sixteenth centuries are considered by the Czechs as the highest point of their history, their most glorious era. Its glory does not rest on victorious wars, on the deeds of their rulers, but on the achievements of both the spirit and hands of the nation. For the nation was then the abode of education and morality, in both of which, in that period, we held our own with other nations. And both were the work of the Hussites alone, for during those two centuries the Catholics in the country numbered scarcely ten per cent. of the population and the Germans still less.

After the battle of Mohacs the Czechs called, in 1526, Ferdinand I of Habsburg to their vacant throne. This was an imprudent act, as was soon discovered, first by the nobility by whom the King was elected, and afterwards by the whole nation. Ferdinand I reigned by Machiavellian methods, and thus succeeded in sowing discord between the nobles and towns and between the Utraquists and Catholics, in order to strengthen his throne at the expense of the liberties of the Estates and to root out the nation's Hussite spirit. In this he received all possible support from both Rome and Spain. Calling Jesuits to Bohemia, he also installed a Catholic archbishop in Prague, the first after a lapse of 130 years. His system of rule was faithfully followed by his successors, and it was in vain that the Czechs tried to obtain a law which would guarantee religious liberty to the Protestants, although they formed the majority of the nation and now consisted of the Utraquists, who, owing to Luther's influence, had long ago broken with Rome for good, and the Bohemian Brethren. Without such a law religious peace in Bohemia was impossible from the moment when, through the influence of the Court, the Spanish-Jesuit party began to gain strength in the country. Finally the Estates understood how to make good use of the quarrels in the Habsburg family and compelled the ailing King Rudolph II to sign, in 1609, a solemn " Letter of Majesty," guaranteeing religious liberty to all. The Spanish ambassadors, however, who were the real representatives of the Habsburg family, feared to give the country a moment's respite, and by altogether unheard-of means kept on provoking the Czechs till they succeeded in driving the unprepared Estates into the rebellion of 1618, which ended in a pitiable defeat on the White Mountain near Prague on November 8th 1620, a day for long fateful for the whole nation. It was a clash of the Catholic with the Protestant world, the shores of which met in Bohemia.

And then there came upon the Czech nation a period of inexpressible evil. The Bohemian State, Protestant up to that time, unable to resist the combined and material intellectual oppression, soon became Roman Catholic throughout. The *Estates*, which till then had constituted the true protection of the country's autonomy, were supplanted by the arbitrariness of the Habsburgs. The Czech language ceased to be the official language. Bohemia became a bilingual (Czecho-German) country, till at last German became the dominant language of the land. Since the wandering of the nations there had not been such changes in our country as those brought about by the Habsburg victor, who confiscated two-thirds of the property of the nobility and of the towns to distribute it among his creatures and foreign military adventurers. The Roman Church put in her claim for a share of the booty in a way even less merciful. The Emperor Ferdinand II preferred to see the Bohemian Kingdom desolated rather than heretic, while Rome desired to have the Czech nation purely Roman Catholic. Thus it came about that Hussitism was proclaimed a crime against the State and the population were converted forcibly by Catholic missionaries and *dragonades* (Jesuits accompanied by dragoons). Some 36,000 families emigrated from Bohemia, Moravia and Silesia rather than accept the yoke of the Roman Church. This partly explains why, after the Thirty Years War, there were barely 800,000 inhabitants left in Bohemia (exclusive of the other Crown lands), while before 1620 she had had fully 2,000,000.

The Jesuits also suppressed all literature, science and the schools. Protestant books were burned at the stake. Moreover, the Jesuits changed the Czech calendar by adding to the patron saints of the country a new saint, John Nepomuk, a fabulous figure but one nevertheless canonized by the Pope. This John was designed to eradicate John Huss from the memory of the people. The Jesuits tried to suppress even the language of the " Králická Bible " by creating a new so-called " St. Wenceslas tongue " (jazyk svato-václav-ský). And nothing could characterize the spiritual decline of the nation more drastically than the circumstance, that up to Maria Theresa's time the schools in Bohemia were attended by only 30,000 children. This in a country which as far back as the fifteenth century flourished with education and prosperity ! After 1627 the Bohemian nation lived spiritually only in exile. Whatever there is of value in Czech literature between 1627–1780, was all written by our exiles living in Germany, Poland and the Netherlands. The most famous of the Czech exiles, *Joh Amos Komenský* (Comènius), (1592–1670), the last bishop of the Bohemian Brotherhood, wandered for more than forty years an exile in foreign lands and it was in a foreign land that he died (in Amsterdam). His activities are specially memorable, because, while he was trying to find allies against Austria he also deliberated all the time how to reform his fellow-countrymen after they should be free again, and this he meant to accomplish by a perfected and organized educational system. While ever having his own nation in his mind, he improved the schools of foreign nations and won the name of a " teacher of nations," by some of his writings, such as " Brána jazyků " (The Gate of Tongues) and the " Didactic " which were translated into all European and, partly, also into Asiatic languages.

In the middle of the eighteenth century the condition of the Czech nation was such that the neighbouring nations considered it already extinct. Yet not even the Habsburg State, that " China of Europe," could resist the pressure of liberal ideas. During the liberal movement which penetrated to us from England and France via Germany, the Bohemian nation began to awaken to a new life. Of all the Habsburgs there is

only one ruler to whom the Czechs are under obliga-
tions—Joseph II, son of Francis of Lorraine and
Maria Theresa, who, himself a man of enlightenment,
demolished by his reforms the old feudal and Roman
Catholic state of Austria and built a new structure in
its stead.   Favouring religious liberty, he stopped the
missionary activity of the Jesuits in Bohemia, freed the
peasants from serfdom and gave his support to schools.

The Czech national revival took place by a process
which could not always be understood in other countries.   Taking advantage of the freedom of scientific
research, historians set to work excavating from the
débris of ages information about events both forgotten
and accursed.   They learned to know both Huss and
the religious Reformation, George of Poděbrad as well
as Komenský.   Simultaneously, the philologists acquainted themselves with the old foundations of the
written language, as they were laid by Huss and Blahoslav.   Moreover, during the period of religious toleration there appeared on the scene the still unburnt books
of the clandestine heretics, of which, in Joseph II's
time, more than 50,000 were counted.   After the
historian and philologist, the idea of revival was taken
up by the poet and journalist.   When the eighteenth
century was merging into the nineteenth, French
revolutionary ideas with their watchwords of Liberty,
Equality and Fraternity, began to resound in the primi-
tive Czech works of fiction of those times.   Under
the pressure of the Holy Alliance reaction the Czechs,
in order to strengthen themselves, made use of modern
methods, printing books and journals, establishing
libraries and museums, taking care of their schools and
turning to scientific labours.   The Czech politician
came on the scene only when the French revolution

of February 1848 began to advance eastwards and set also Vienna, Prague and Budapest aflame.

It was in Prague that the revolution broke out first (on the 11th of March). Although it was suppressed (the Bohemian peasant alone gained his freedom by the abolition of socage) and punished by the stifling reaction of the years 1850–1860, the Czech politician was no longer absent from the Austrian tribunal. The revival of the Czech nation is especially interesting for the reason that it was accomplished without the participation of the so-called higher classes, for the Czech nobility had been already Germanized in the seventeenth century.

It must not be thought that the political Czech movement in the nineteenth century was revolutionary. The Czech politicians, even as late as 1848, pinned their hopes to the Throne and Government and subsequently offered to co-operate in building up a strong Austria, if the latter would be just to the Czech nation. Even the programme of Bohemian State rights, which became well known all over Europe, despite its demanding the restoration of the State of Bohemia— thus the uniting of Bohemia, Moravia and Silesia— was a conservative programme. It was put forward by the Czech aristocracy (Count Martinic) and the leader of the nation of that time, Dr. Rieger. But it was the Habsburg policy itself which drove the Czechs into opposition. The Crown shared the sway over the State with the German and Magyar minorities, although the Bohemian lands paid the most taxes and although the Austrian State was created in 1526 as a triple empire : German—Bohemian—Hungarian, with equal rights for all the three components. Only occasionally did the Czech tactics assume a revolutionary character, but never consistently or permanently. After sixteen years of passive politics, from 1862 to 1878, when we did not attend the Vienna Parliament and thus gained, unjustly, the reputation of implacable rebels, there was only a small party of radicals who advocated a continued policy of obstruction and the breaking up of the Parliament, and this with small success. And even when the conservative Old Czech (Rieger's) party was replaced by the Young Czechs (Sladkovský and the Grégr brothers), the Czech political parties were always ready to discuss with Austria the demands for equal rights and such a degree of autonomy as was obtained by the Magyars in the sixties.

A new national programme was laid before the nation by T. G. Masaryk—a programme of work in order to gain inner strength. In this programme education and moral principles occupied the first place, political activity coming second. Yet neither did Masaryk's policy advocate revolution at first. It differed from the official, so-called "positive," politics in that Masaryk despised the dynasty and tried rather to raise in the Austrian Parliament such a majority of all the nationalities represented there as would put new life into the decayed empire, do away with absolutism and transform Austria into a progressive State. The opposition standpoint was taken by Masaryk in 1907, after his second election to the Parliament, and he gradually raised his programme to a revolutionary one, when Austria-Hungary entangled herself in the World War. Even if, at first, he adhered to Palacký's motto that Austria is necessary to Europe, yet he had already, in his essay on Palacký's idea of the nation (1898), declared that between the Czech and Austrian idea there was a difference of principles. From Palacký he deviated also in that he believed in the possibility of Czech independence, should democracy and socialistic tendencies in Europe grow more powerful. The revolution he recognized, the longer he thought of it, as perfectly justified from the point of view of morality.

When, in 1914, the war broke out, Masaryk considered it a favourable moment not only for thinking of the revolution but also for bringing it about. Accurately estimating the situation of the warring nations, he became certain that both Germany and Austria would be defeated and that military and diplomatic co-operation with the Entente nations would bring liberty to both the Czechs and Slovaks. Armed revolution, which the Czechs could not make at home, they made beyond the frontiers. This was why Masaryk laid such stress on independent Czech armies in France, in Russia and in Italy. At the same time he formed personal connections with politicians and governments abroad in order to gain favour for the Czech idea. The Czech legions in Russia especially subsequently proved to be of great service to the Entente.

Thus Komenský's belief that a time would come when the conduct of Czech affairs would be restored to the hands of the nation, came true. The month of October 1918 restored it to the Czech nation—it brought even more than the preceding generations dreamt of and of what the generation then living had only spoken of with trepidation : the Czech State became a Republic and was supplemented by Slovakia, that is to say, by that part of the Czech nation which the Magyars had held in subjection for a thousand years.

The Republic has now about 14 millions of inhabitants. Of this total the Czecho-Slovaks (this name we adopted as a compliment to the Slovak branch) number over 9 millions, the Germans over 3 millions, the Magyars about 700,000, etc.

The restoration of the Bohemian State is felt by the Czechs now living to be not only an act of historic justice, but every individual feels it a personal happiness to have lived long enough to see it.   But from this feeling of happiness there also arises, for a free nation, a feeling of responsibility and the duty of each and all to show themselves worthy, in a free state, of their freedom.   The road to this is indicated by the foreword which stands at the head of the constitutional charter : " It will be our endeavour to see that this constitution and all the laws of our country be kept in the spirit of our history as well as in the spirit of those modern principles embodied in the idea of self-determination, for we desire to take our place in the Family of Nations, as a member at once cultured, peace-loving, democratic and progressive."

Possessing a country practically self-supporting and adapted equally for agriculture and industry, the Czechs intend to work for their material and intellectual welfare.   Having no intention of increasing their domain or making any new conquests, all they wish for is a policy of peace and universal brotherhood. For there is scarcely anyone in Europe who would not know that there is here once more a " people without a sword."   Of course, they know how to defend themselves, and are capable of resistance should their independence be attacked.   It was predicted by Ernest Denis, that Komenský's heirs would also be the heirs of Žižka.   The proof of this was furnished by our legionaries. The inner policy of the country will devote itself to matters of culture and mental progress. There being now practically no illiterates, the aim of the Czechs is to work for as high a cultural development of the nation as possible. The Czecho-Slovak Republic has a constitutional government, its finances are the best ordered of all the States in Central Europe, and despite some difficulties still caused by the Germans, Magyars and the clerical Slovaks, the State is fast advancing towards her own consolidation and in international esteem. The traditional democracy of the Czechs is expressed in these three words : Huss, Komenský, Masaryk. All three, although born of the common stock, have made the Czech name famous.

II

John Huss and the Hussite Doctrines

THE Bohemian nation was destined not only
to proclaim, but also to put into effect, the
revolt against the omnipotence of the
Roman Church in the mediæval era, and against her
supreme rule over the hearts and minds of men.
History calls this revolt *Hussitism*, after its outstanding
representative, John Huss. The Bohemian movement was at first purely religious, and only in its subsequent progress did it grow into a national revolution,
carried through by John Žižka with his people's army.
Just as the Huss "heresy" has its significance in
Church history, so has Žižka's warfare in political
history, for by the secession of the Czechs a breach
was made in the existing unity of the Christian world
—a breach which was later further widened by the
reformations of Luther and Calvin.

The causes of the religious resistance to the Roman
Church are well known. In some localities they were
theoretical, merely representing objections to some
Church dogma, but in other places they were more of
a moral and practical character, as the faithful were
irritated by the circumstance that the Church had
relinquished the ideal of Apostolic perfection, and
desired secular power over the Christian bodies rather

than spiritual authority over their souls. The blame for this was put on the Popes. Literature, from the twelfth century on, expresses its opposition to Rome, and from about the same period the unity of the Church was threatened by sects. Thus the Albigensian and Waldensian sects, the first in the neighbourhood of the town of Albi in southern France, the second in Provence and Piedmont, seceded. The herald of the latter sect was not a theologian, but the rich merchant Valdus, of Lyons. Giving up his wealth, he became a preacher, like the merchant's son, Francis of Assisi. He preached a morally strict life, and, above all, poverty. The Waldensians blamed the Church for accepting a present from the Emperor Constantine, for abandoning spiritual life, and finding her pleasure in worldly life, riches, and dominion. Once they had commenced to reason they decided to condemn both the Church of Rome and her hierarchy, and declared that in their opinion even a layman could preach, because a good layman was a priest too. They abolished the death penalty, rejected the State power and military authority (for it is the army upon which the power of the Church is founded), and also the oath. The Waldensians found adherents even beyond the Alps in Germany, in Austria, also in southern Bohemia, and finally appeared in England. (The German peasant rebellion on the Weser was suppressed in 1234.)

The discord in the Church steadily grew during the so-called Babylonian imprisonment of the Popes in Avignon (1305–1378), and still more when, in 1378, the papal schism broke out, when there were two Popes at once and finally three, who execrated each other in hearty fashion. And it was always human reason, which, both from the universities and from the monasteries, protested against the Roman dogmas, and it was always, too, the human heart which could find neither rest nor spiritual consolation in the Churches, for it was piety and not theological teachings that it sought.

Thus when the revolt against Rome broke out in Bohemia, there was nothing exclusively Czech in it, just as there was nothing exclusively English in Wyclif's opposition In reading capacious books in the thirteenth and fourteenth centuries, we find that neither Wyclif nor Huss were the first disturbers of the Church's peace, but that there was, long before Huss' time, much violent heresy uttered, the like of which Huss did not approach even at the close of his life. Huss became memorable because he did not retract like others when pressed by the Church, but carried the consequences of his opinions to their practical conclusion. And the Czech nation deserves credit because it stood by Huss faithfully and rose in defence of his principles against the whole world of those times.

All Europe was then volcanic ground. The Papal imprisonment at Avignon still continued and already, in perhaps every European country, spiritual unrest was rampant. A new phenomenon in history was that suddenly the voice of the people was heard, the voice of the broad masses, as we now express it. The people entered upon the historical stage at the end of the fourteenth and the beginning of the fifteenth century. The people it was also that was called upon to judge and arbitrate in the papal quarrels and the disputes of the Popes with the secular rulers. Having long deliberated over Church affairs which did not at all agree with its own ideas of them, the people was at last forced to think when asked for its verdict.

There was nothing revolutionary about the spiritual unrest in the second half of the fourteenth century. It signified that the best heads were giving much thought to the reform of the Church. Against these notable thinkers there existed almost everywhere narrow-minded members of the hierarchy, whether the Pope with the cardinals or the Archbishop with the bishops, who saw nothing in the opinions of the thinkers but attacks upon the Church or a hostility which could sweep them from their elevated and lucrative positions.

Two countries attract the attention of historians seeking the beginnings of heresy—England and Bohemia.

They both deserve attention. But it is interesting from our—the Czech—standpoint, to examine the volcanic soil of both countries and to compare the manner in which the reforms manifested themselves in England and Bohemia. They begin almost simultaneously.

Wyclif made his literary appearance in 1356 when he was 32 years old. His work, *The Last Age of the Church*, occupies itself with prophesies. A great pestilence was then raging. In England, Wyclif, supporting himself by the predictions of a certain abbot and an abbess, announced in Old Testament terms and similes the approaching downfall and end of the Church. In 1364 he had a dispute with the Mendicant Friar Woodhall regarding appointments to ecclesiastical dignities and appealed to the Pope.

But before the Pope could answer, Wyclif began to think about another matter, and ended by opposing the Pope. That is to say, Pope Urban VI reminded England in 1365, of the payment which the hapless King John Lackland agreed to send him every year, when, beset by difficulties, he accepted the English throne in fief from the Pope, thus becoming his vassal. This payment, as is well known, weighed heavily on England, besides greatly humiliating her pride. Wyclif declared against it, gaining thereby the favour of the Court, the Parliament and the people. In this sense Wyclif's bold stand was likewise both national and nationalistic.

When the Parliament, not long afterwards, decided that the clergy should not hold high secular offices, Wyclif wrote two treatises in support of this decision. And he came out in the same manner against that papal abuse—the bestowing of English prebends on incapable foreigners. Having gained the favour of King Edward III, Wyclif was sent, in 1374, to Bruges in the Low Countries to negotiate with the papal envoys, but returned without accomplishing anything. All that he brought back with him was the conviction, which he did not conceal from the King, that that proud secular priest in Rome was the most damnable extortioner of money in Christendom. The King then gave Wyclif the living of Aust and the Parliament took a stand against the Pope.

In 1377 began the citing of Wyclif before the spiritual courts. Unfortunately for Wyclif, the new King, Richard II, was a shaking reed who removed his protecting hand from him. The high clergy examined Wyclif's works and collected his private utterances and found heresy in them. Wyclif wrote in answer several defences which became celebrated in the future, as they represent both his teaching and his theological character. In January 1382 a solemn clerical synod assembled in London and rejected twenty-four of Wyclif's theses. Wyclif was deprived of his office, but gained both in fame and the love of the people. Summoned to appear at Rome before the court tribunal, he did not go and, in December 1384, died.

It is necessary to outline, briefly at least, the main teachings of Wyclif, because it should be known in what his influence upon our Hussitism consisted. He accepted the convention of the Church according to the view expressed by St. Augustine. The Church is not the aggregate of all those who confess it, but of those only whom God predestined to salvation, while those whom He knows in advance to be lost can never be members of the true Church of Christ. From that Wyclif concluded that there is no difference between priest and bishop or between a clergyman in general and a layman. The chosen, predestined layman is the true son of God, even if he be not consecrated by a bishop. Another of his teachings was that the only authority in matters of faith is the Gospel, and that in the Gospel there is nothing about the veneration of the saints or pictures, that there are no masses for the dead, no purgatory, nor the seven sacraments. And because Wyclif found from what sources the clergy drew their chief power over the laity, he struck at the doctrine that a priest could, by some conjuring trick, transform the host into the real body and blood of Christ. According to Wyclif bread remains ordinary bread even after its consecration by the priest, and only figuratively or sacramentally becomes the body of Christ. Thus Wyclif opposed the notorious doctrine of transubstantiation, which afterwards played a great

rôle in the Bohemian, German and Swiss reformations.

Wyclif's teaching gave rise to the English sect of the
Lollards, who, after the reformer's death, drew from
his words further conclusions, as, for example, preaching by laymen, zeal in opposing priestly abuses,
rejection of celibacy, the nun's vow, war and the death
penalty. There also arose among the Lollards the
teaching that the effect of the sacrament administered
by the priest to believers is subject to the priest's moral
character, that a sacrament administered by a bad priest
has no saving effect. The Lollards were bloodily
suppressed by the State and the Church.

At about the same time that Wyclif came into conflict with the Mendicant Friars the Church reform
movement began in Bohemia. With us its leaders
were preachers and men of learning.

The first preacher in Prague was Conrad Waldhauser, a German, called to Prague by the Emperor
Charles IV himself. Side by side with him worked a
Moravian Czech, Milič, who in 1363 resigned his
lucrative canonry at Prague to become a mere ascetic
preacher, and continued in Waldhauser's footsteps
after the latter's death. Some of the theologians
intervened with their learning, as, for instance, Magister Matthews of Genoa, the " master of Paris." They
all met with resistance on the part of the hierarchy
and became suspect as heretics. Milič, who lived a
life of self-denial and brought about a great religious
movement, established a house for the Magdalenes,
popularly called Bethlehem. He over and over again
reiterated the opinion that Antichrist would soon
appear in the world, calling even Charles IV by that
dreaded name and pointing his finger at him during a

festival sermon.   While in Rome he was arrested for
heresy on the accusation of the Roman cardinals.   A
second accusation of the same kind was made against
him by the Prague monks.   In 1473 he went to Avignon to clear himself of the charge of heresy and his
domestic opponents rejoiced at the idea that he would
be burnt at last.   He succeeded, however, in clearing
himself, but died before his case was ended at Avignon
in 1374.   Magister Janovský had to contend with
similar opposition.   He had to retract his imaginary
errors twice, but did not abandon them.   The most
progress in heresy of them all was made by the priest
Jacob of Kaplice.

Yet what surprises one most is the fact that on
Bohemian soil the same opinions grew up as in England.   If we pick out, from the works of the Bohemian
preachers and theologians, their anti-church views,
they will together give us nearly all that was preached
by Huss.   Beginning with Waldhauser, the anti-
clerical view and the doctrine of the common priesthood of laymen, i.e., the demand that no distinction
should be made between the common people and the
priesthood in regard to frequent or even daily communion, gained ground.   Even the most conservative
of them all, Magister Vojtěch, condemned simony,
Milič and Janovský still more, of course.   They all
reject the worship of the saints, veneration of pictures,
of relics and masses for the dead ; one among them
even the worship of the Virgin Mary.   Janovský
opposed a number of Church rules, because they con-
tradicted the Scriptures and declared the papacy to be a
usurpation by the Bishop of Rome.   The Pope was to
him the source of all the Church abuses and sins,
especially of simony.   Some of our people had   the

same conception of the Church as Wyclif, i.e., that there are, properly, two Churches, one visible and the other invisible. The number of our moralists was also increased by a layman, a yeoman of Southern Bohemia, Thomas of Štitné, who wrote, to the amazement of the orthodox clergy, his book in the Czech language, a procedure which in itself smacked of heresy to them. There is only a single doctrine of Wyclif which, up to the end of the fourteenth century, could not be found among the Bohemians—and that was his teaching upon transubstantiation. This shows that, on a soil of the same conditions, the same species of plants will grow ; the resemblance between England and Bohemia in this respect is remarkable indeed.

And yet there was a very substantial difference between the English heretic and the Bohemian heretics. Wyclif's opposition to the Church was due to worldly and national reasons, as well as to a scientific knowledge of Church history. On the other hand, the reasons prompting the Bohemian heretics were purely religious, they sprang from a desire to reform society by the deepening of moral life. Our reformers got involuntarily on another, not Church, ground, and dogmatic deviations were not the object, but the mere consequences of their endeavours.

In John Huss the Bohemian movement was depicted in its most vivid and illustrative form and in his person it also ripened to explosion. From the appearance of the first preacher, Waldhauser, forty years passed before the appearance of Huss.

Huss, a sturdy countryman from the Šumava region, of peasant parentage, studied in Prague both at the intermediate schools and the University, became, in 1396, a master of arts, and began to lecture at the

University.   Entering the Church in 1400, it was his
desire to become a doctor of theology, so that he could
lecture at the theological faculty.   Of his youth we
know only what he says about himself in some of his
works.   His poverty he recalls in his later years in
these words : " . . . when I was a hungry little scholar,
making myself a spoon out of my bread, I ate my peas
till I also ate up the spoon."   He earned his living by
singing and ministering in the churches of Prague :
" It was a pity, but what could I, sinful as I was, do !
The priests and scholars declaim and sing for hours ;
even as I did, when I was a scholar and sung the vigilia
with the others, so we sung just to get done with it ;
for the money was taken by others, who raked and
ploughed with us.   Woe to us if both of us shall not
repent."

Such were the queer morals of those times, when the
churches could be desecrated by vulgar plays of all
kinds.   The second Christmas holiday was celebrated
by the scholars with unheard-of gaieties : " And what
of the open levity they commit in the church, putting
on masks (even I in my youth once put on a mask,
sinner that I am !), who could describe all of them in
Prague ?   Making a bishop of a wag of a scholar, they
seated him on a she-ass with his face towards her tail,
led him into a church to hear the mass ; and put before
him a bowl of soup and a can or a pitcher of beer, and
held this before him while he ate.   And he, seeing the
incense offered at the altar, lifts his leg and cries in a
lusty voice : Boo !   And the scholars carry large
torches before him instead of candles and go from altar
to altar thus burning incense.   Then it could be seen
that all the scholars had turned their fur capots inside
out and were dancing in the church ; and the people

look at it and laugh, and think all that is holy or true, because they have it in their rubric, that is, in their regulations."

When consecrated, however, Huss began to think of his calling. A conversion took place. He erased himself " from that crazy rubric " and repented even that he used to play chess, that he enjoyed wearing the showy sacerdotal robe and that he preached in the churches of Prague. Of Huss' learning we know nothing special, but of his piety, his conscientious scruples and his eloquence as a preacher a good deal. But his learning could not have been slight for he was, in 1402, elected rector of the University.

And thus the year 1402 is a great event in Huss' life. He was elected not only rector but also preacher in the Bethlehem chapel. The distinction was just as significant as the mission, for this chapel was not a parish, but, we might say, something like a religious lecture hall. It was built in 1391 by a Prague merchant and a country squire, that the word of God be preached there in Czech exclusively. This stipulation unveils to some extent the nationalistic conditions in Prague at that time.

Ever since Milič's time the Archbishop of Prague hampered the preachers in every possible way, going even so far as to forbid the sermons altogether. Yet the Czech sermons were preached just the same, although clandestinely. The foundation charter of the Bethlehem chapel distinctly states that it was intended to remedy the lack of sermons, especially of Czech sermons.

The majority of the parishes were either in the hands of German priests or such of Czech nationality as were bitterly hostile to the moral tendencies initiated by

Waldhauser and Huss. The Bethlehem chapel was built by zealots and became a stronghold of the Church reform party. This shows what progress in piety was made by the Czechs in the last forty years, when even laymen did not begrudge sacrifices for an edifice undoubtedly costly.

And thus the year 1402 signifies for both Hussite history and for Huss personally a moment of vast importance. In the person of Huss were united both the reformation tendencies which were then convulsing Europe—the learned and the popular course, the complaint of reason against more than one of the Church's doctrines and the revolt of human hearts against the depravity of the Church, that neglected both piety and faith.

At the University Huss taught the young Czech intelligentsia ; in the Bethlehem chapel he spoke to the burghers and nobles, to the artisans and labourers. If we cannot get, from the printed sermons, an idea of the oratorical value of Huss' sermons, their essential part we can recognize easily. As a speaker Huss knew how to hold the attention of his audience by an animated delivery during which he asked his hearers oratorical questions, answering them, of course, himself, and touching in this manner the burning topics of the day ; he also frequently addressed men, women or girls of his audience, pointing his finger at one or another of them as if speaking to him or her alone. When, in later years, he once noticed among his hearers a disguised spying monk, he did not hesitate to call to him : " Thou fellow in the hood there, write up what thou hast heard and carry it to the archbishop ! " Huss' language shows a master, being both elegant and simple, pathetic and modest at the same time.

But it is unusually rich, picturesque and vivacious. Even when it flows like a quiet river, it is filled with the rays of a speaker's wit, with popular proverbs and fragments or allusions from the common songs of that period. There are also lengthy analyses of theological subjects, but we can hardly blame a man of the fifteenth century for speaking in the manner of his age. There are many even in our nation who begin to read Huss' sermons and writings in general and lay them aside disappointed. For they expected some sort of revolutionary contents, mottoes about liberty, equality and fraternity or rebellious socialist principles, and, behold, there was nothing of the kind. Only very simple and, of course, also impressive, fervent expositions of the essential truths of the Gospel, of the Lord's prayer, an analysis of the Ten Commandments, an instruction about the sacraments and sins and all that every Christian should know. For Huss observed that the people heard religious words but were ignorant of their sense ; they thought that the Holy Trinity was some woman saint ! But one deep feature appears in all the sermons and works of Huss, both Czech and Latin : the character of the native moralist tradition, of the Milič kind. Huss follows in Milič's footsteps.

That Huss was doing well at the University we can see from his popularity with his colleagues the professors, as well as with the students, although he was none too lenient with them at the academic examinations. We know a number of Huss' lectures at least by their titles, and a further number have been completely preserved to us. Thus the *Gesta Christi*, read at the faculty of art, shows a thorough knowledge of the subject. That Huss also paid attention to secular

literature is proved by the circumstance that already
on September 30th 1398, the day of " St. Jerome the
Slav," he finished, with his own hand, copies of some
of Wyclif's philosophical treatises.   With what joy
and understanding he read them we know from his
marginal remarks, both serious and humorous.   Wyclif's philosophical works were known at Prague
University long before his theological ones. *De
materia et forma*, for instance, is that work of Wyclif's
into which the following remark was written by Huss :
" O Wycleff, Wycleff, nejednomu ty hlavu zvikleš "
(oh, Wycleff, Wycleff, thou wilt turn the head of more
than one).   In another work (*De deis*), he feared a
reader of less mental depth would not understand, so
he added : " Nechvátaj non intelligentibus dávati "
(be not in haste to impart to the ignorant).   And full
of joy that Wyclif comprehended the mystery of the
Holy Trinity, he sighed devoutly : " God grant Wyclif
the Kingdom of Heaven."

   But there is also a new note to be detected in Huss'
preaching and teaching, something not observed in
any of his predecessors, not even in Štitný, when he
defended himself against reproaches for writing in
Czech.   When Huss learned that " the proud or
stupid slander me and grumble because I write in
Czech," he replied that it were " better to read good
Czech works in the castles and indeed anywhere, than
to go about gossiping, causing quarrels and committing
whoredom.   Even St. Paul, to whomsoever he wrote
his epistles, wrote in their tongue, in Hebrew to Jews,
in Greek to Greeks.   St. Jerome wrote to old women
and explained writings from an unknown tongue. . . .
The more intelligent will understand it, and thus the
Czech tongue is as precious to God as the Latin."   By

Salue sancte cinis, Christi salue inclyte martyr.
Husse decus patriæ, luxq; Bohæmigenûm.

JOHN HUSS.

[*To face p.* 48

this the problem of the popular tongue in the Church was, in principle, solved.

In Huss' time there also cropped up another, more serious, problem, the problem of nationality, that is to say, the strife between the Czechs and the Germans, a problem which, in the reign of Václav IV, was aggravated by political circumstances. Anyway, the conditions in Prague, and Bohemia in general, began to shape themselves differently from those prevailing in the reign of his father. For, in the first place, the Bohemian nation became a factor at the University and bore with impatience the unjust representation there, which gave to the foreign " nations " three votes (as a matter of fact, they were all Germans, although a Saxon, Bavarian and Polish nation is spoken of), while the Czechs or Bohemians had only one. The first quarrel on this account broke out in 1380, the second in 1388. On the surface these quarrels seemed to be only secular, but the real dividing factor between Czech and German was the movement for reform.

Waldhauser had gained no followers in Prague. Speaking once of his teachers, Huss did not name a single German professor, and it is known that the Bohemian masters adhered to philosophical realism, while the Germans were nominalists. Such things interest us very little nowadays, but we must admit that realism was progressive. Already in 1401 a German sermon was a rarity in Prague. The more the German strata of the population kept aloof from the religious ferment the more pronouncedly adverse became the Bohemians to them.

The political conditions of the country furnished the Bohemian party with much combustible matter. The heritage of Charles IV developed into a great hegemony of the clergy all over the Czech State. The Church was, in the true sense of the word, a state within a state, and in the violent conflict between King Václav IV and the Archbishop Jenstejn, the King lost. The outcome of this conflict was that the Archbishop, with the help of his vicar-general John of Pomuk, succeeded in preventing the King from establishing new bishoprics in Bohemia (1393). Besides the hierarchy, the power of the great lords, the higher nobility also successfully competed with, and even often triumphed over, the royal Government. The nobles weakened the King's authority to such an extent that they were blamed by the national party for Václav's loss of the German throne. Moreover they, like the King's brother Sigmund, even dared to capture and imprison him. The relations of the Church to the State and their inner conditions were continuously in the minds of the Bohemians of those times.

Huss, from being a spokesman of religious reform, was gradually becoming in addition the spokesman of the national party. The German historian Bezold has rightly observed that : " The energetic stand taken by the Czech nationality against the German would never have been possible without the flame of religious enthusiasm. It was necessary that the Bohemian should become a ' Warrior of God, the German an enemy of the divine law, so that their fight could become a life and death struggle.' "

When the Germans of the Empire elected Rupprecht as a rival king to King Václav IV, and Rupprecht began, in 1401, a war during which the Saxon army penetrated as far as Prague, and the Bohemian nobles and the Archbishop allied themselves with him, the Czechs felt this to be a national humiliation.

It was then that Huss delivered the following sermon in the St. Michael's Church :

" The Czechs are worse than the dogs and snakes, because the dog defends the bed he is lying on and if another dog would try to drive him away, he would fight with him, and so would the snake ; but the Germans are oppressing us and also seizing all the offices in Bohemia and we are silent. According to law, even according to the law of God and from natural instinct, the Czechs should be the first in all the offices of the Bohemian Kingdom, the same as the French in the French Kingdom and the Germans in their own lands, so that the Czech knows how to rule his subjects and the German the German. But will it profit that a Czech, ignorant of the German language, is a pastor or bishop in Germany ? Faith, he will count there for as much as would for a flock a dumb dog incapable of barking, and so much good is a German to us."

The later period has left us more of Huss' patriotic expressions. He wished, in particular, that the lords should take care that the Czech language did not perish. " If a Czech married a German woman, that the children should learn Czech at once and not duplicate the languages. For double languages are nothing but envy, dissension, provocation and quarrel. Therefore Emperor Charles of sacred memory, the King of Bohemia, bade the people of Prague have their children learn Czech and, in their town-hall, which the Germans call Rathhaus, also to speak and to litigate in Czech. And in truth, as Nehemiah, hearing the Jewish children talk among themselves half Azot and not knowing Hebrew, he flogged and beat them for that, so now deserve to be flogged the people of Prague and also other Czechs, who talk half Czech and half German. . . ."

From 1402 to 1408 Huss preached in the Bethlehem chapel without hindrance, even enjoying the favour of the Archbishop Zbyněk of Hasenburg. The discord and unrest came from the University, and were caused by Wyclif's theological works, which in 1403 were brought from Oxford to Prague. There was a conflict on their account between the Czechs and the Germans. It was the German professor Hübner who suddenly laid before the Archbishop's chapter Wyclif's twenty-four articles, which had been condemned by the London synod, and twenty-one other suspicious articles. The chapter sent them to the University to be adjudged there. The Rector at that time was the German Harasser. At the university council the Germans declared unanimously for the condemnation of the articles, while the Bohemians defended them as being orthodox. Huss was not among the first, but only became exasperated when a Czech colleague called his attention to some articles which had been falsified. " Such falsifiers," he said, " should have been punished by death rather than those two merchants recently, who falsified saffron."

The Archbishop remained impartial for a long time, and his diocese was quiet. But all at once the German professors and the chapter succeeded in arousing the Archbishop, so that he prohibited the preaching of all extra sermons in Prague and the singing of Bohemian songs in the Bethlehem chapel. The Germans importuned even the papal chair and the King with their complaints about Wyclif. At the King's wish, in 1408, the Archbishop made a solemn declaration in the synod that he found no heresy in Prague, that was as far as the Holy Communion is concerned.

Immediately afterwards, however, the priests of Prague sent in complaints against Huss, to the effect that he was inciting, in the Bethlehem chapel, the people against the clergy, whom he reproached with extorting from the people pay for confessions, for sacraments, for the sacrifices, funerals, ringing of the bells, etc. In these complaints there were the first hints at heresy. In 1409 the Archbishop issued a ban upon the Wyclifites and the owners of his books, and in the same year he accused Huss directly in Rome, when he was summoned there himself for favouring the heretics. In 1410 the Archbishop had all Wyclif's books he could get hold of burnt in the courtyard of his palace to the ringing of bells and the singing of *Te Deums*. The prelates and chosen clergy added lustre to this ceremony.

In the meantime a passionate conflict broke out between the King and the Archbishop regarding neutrality towards the three popes of that period, and by this state of affairs Huss' condition was greatly aggravated. It was followed by a ban against Huss, by disturbances in Prague on account of indulgences, and by the voluntary departure of Huss from Prague to exile in the country. This exile is memorable because in the years 1412–1414 Huss wrote his best book in Czech and preached to the common people in Southern and Western Bohemia. The purport of the complaints the priests made against him he formulated briefly and accurately thus : " In the year 1402 after the birth of the Son of God, Magister John Huss, born at Husinec, began to preach in Bethlehem. And in general he says that as long as he was preaching to the lords, knights and pages, to the burghers and trades-

men, they all praised and were kind to him. But
when he attacked the priests and the Pope and other
classes of the clergy, many of his adherents left him.
And the Pope owing to the accusations made by the
priests against him began to summon him to Rome
and issued a ban against him."

How clear that is ! Huss preached of the depravity
of Rome as well as of the clergy and monks. He spoilt
the priest's revenues. Therefore he had to be silenced.
But silenced he could be only as a heretic. For that
he had done any injustice to the Pope and the clergy
could not be proved against him. The clergy of
Prague, in particular, had the worst reputation. The
visitation of the Prague parishes, undertaken by Archbishop Arnošt of Pardubice while Emperor Charles
IV was still living, disclosed horrible conditions.
They were so disgraceful and painful, that to this day
nobody has ever dared to publish them in print. And
under his successors it was no better. What Huss
himself experienced and what he wrote of licentiousness,
gambling, drunkenness and simony, surpasses all
belief. We can, however, imagine what it must have
been, even without these proofs. Prague had in the
reign of Charles IV, about 70,000 to 80,000 inhabitants. But there were 50 parishes, 27 non-parochial
churches and 25 monasteries. And every parish
supported about 20 priests, at Vyšehrad there were 100
and at Hradčany 300. How many rich priests lived
in Prague besides that, although they should have lived
in the country, and how many held temporal positions
is unknown. Of these secular priests Huss writes in
one of his works : " Behold, the burgrave a priest ; a
priest at the land registry, a priest judging ; a priest,
estate manager ; a priest in the kitchen, and the clerk,

also a priest. And if the beadles only received bigger pay, the priest would become a beadle too." People were so afraid of the priests (says the historian of Prague, V. V. Tomek) that a proverb of that time utters the warning, " Have nought to do with a priest, but, shouldst thou insult him, better kill him at once, otherwise he will never give thee rest ! "

The chronicler says that Huss was deserted by many. This happened in 1411 and 1412. The Council of Pisa, which was designed to abolish the double papacy, increased it to a trinity. Although the new Pope, Alexander V, took possession of Rome, Gregory XII found protection in the Kingdom of Naples, and Benedict XIII of Avignon refused to yield. King Václav IV was therefore compelled by political conditions to recognize Alexander V and to force also Archbishop Zbyněk to recognize him. Not so Huss. When, disobeying the Archbishop, he did not cease to preach, the Archbishop laid him under an interdict and caused Huss to be called to account in Rome. In 1411 a ban was sent again from Rome because Huss did not appear there. Still more turbulent was the year 1412, in which Huss took a bold stand against the indulgences then sold in Prague, the proceeds of which Alexander's successor, John XXIII, proposed to use in financing a crusade against the King of Naples. It was at that time that Huss was left by two men who up to a short time before had been among the fiercest champions of Wyclif—Stanislaus of Znojmo and Stephan Páleč, Huss' most intimate friend.

Leaving Prague, Huss wrote a good deal in Czech at Kozi Hrádek, namely his *Postilla*, and *About the Church*. To him the Church was an invisible society of human beings predestined to salvation. The administration of the Church was to be in accord with the Scriptures.

The papacy Huss declared to be of worldly origin ; to him the real head of the Church is Christ. It is the duty of the temporal authorities to maintain discipline among the clergy. A Christian should oppose false orders. Both the temporal and spiritual authorities, if obdurate in sin, lose their power before God.

In this book there were many anti-Church doctrines. Huss knew it well but felt satisfied that the Church was in error, not he. Many people feared for his fate when he decided to go to Constance. When Huss was leaving Prague his admirer, Andrew Polák, said to him, " God go with thee. It seems to me that thou wilt return no more ! "

In 1414 a Council met in Constance in order to reform the Church in both head and limbs, to dispose of the question of the relation of the Church councils to the Pope, and to remove other serious disorders from which the Church was suffering.

How irreconcilably the two worlds were opposed to each other in their quarrels on the home soil was never so clearly shown as in Constance, where Huss went voluntarily, in 1414, to clear himself and his nation of the charge of heresy. They are wellnigh incredible, these animosities by which the Council continued to maltreat Huss, and shame will always accompany the breach of faith by Sigmund, who betrayed him. Equally shameful was the mendacity of the accusers, who did not shrink from uttering before the council such nonsense as that Huss pretended to be the fourth person of the Divinity. However, we may pass over these matters, though they were the very things that excited a large part of the nation to the

utmost, especially the nobility, who voiced their protest at the diet in Prague. What became a part of the
world's history were the principles for which Huss
came into conflict with the Council.

Although Huss had kept on asking for a public
hearing before the holy fathers ever since November
1414, he was not examined publicly until the fifth,
seventh and eighth day of June 1415. But these
hearings were only such as to comply with the form
of the process. In reality, a sentence prepared before-
hand was brought to the first hearing. And the
condemnation of Wyclif's works, on May 4th 1415,
was for Huss a portent that excluded any hope.

On June 5th the Council listened to the reading of
extracts from Huss' works. Forty-five articles, all of
them considered objectionable and heretic, were read.
Huss defended himself by accusing the compiler of the
complaints of detaching his (Huss') utterances from
their context and giving them a false meaning, and of
imputing to him views which he had never either held
or preached. But the judges cried to him to abstain
from evasions and to reply to the individual sentence,
either yes or no. It should have been sufficient for
him that the Council declared such and such views
erroneous. And here Huss formulated, for the first
time, his standpoint in regard to the Council. " I am
ready humbly to retract anything that shall be proved
to me to be erroneous according to the Scriptures."

During his second examination, on June 7th, Huss
reiterated his standpoint, completing it with the asser-
tion that it was more correct to appeal to Christ than
to the Pope. King Sigmund, impatient that Huss
created difficulties for him with the Council, warned
Huss with the words : " I advise thee to retract and

to submit to the Council in everything. If thou wilt do that, a small penance will wash off thy guilt. If thou wilt not do so, know that I shall not defend a hardened heretic and rather will light the stake with my own hand." " God be my witness," replied Huss, " that I shall not abide by my opinions obstinately, but will gladly change them if I am shown better." This second hearing was the stormiest of all. Peter d'Ailli assailed Huss with harsh language, and Páleč lied deliberately, the noise being so great at one time that it was even impossible for Huss' wellwishers to make themselves heard. Huss exclaimed sadly : " I thought that there would be more honesty, more kind- ness and a better order in this body than there is ! "

At the third examination the Council told Huss for the last time to submit unconditionally in all that the Council might decide on ; Huss replied that he never preached some of the things he was accused off and therefore could not retract them if he were not to bring the suspicion upon himself that he did preach them after all ; that he did preach others, as he considered them to be right, but would retract even them if he received better advice on them. " I beg for God's sake that I be not compelled to lie and abjure articles which have never been in my heart." " To advise thee better," replied Peter d'Ailli irritably. " The advice backed by sixty or more doctors of Divinity is : Huss is to acknowledge his errors contained in the articles to which he has held fast to this moment ; he is to abjure the said articles and is to swear that he will no more profess nor preach them ; and, finally, he is publicly to retract them and preach to the contrary."

This was no advice ; this was a sentence.

So it was certainly understood by the Cardinal

Zarabella of Florence. He had, under the profound impression of the trial, promised Huss that he would elaborate a formula of retractation of the articles complained of, in a manner acceptable to Huss.

After this third examination Huss was doomed. It had never been known before, for anybody to refuse unconditional obedience to the Pope or a Council. The Council could not therefore accede to Huss' presumption, which it regarded as impudence and the obduracy of a heretic. Huss was, at that moment, the first human being in the Middle Ages to refuse to obey an authority till then supreme and omnipotent. Nevertheless, the Council deigned to make a last effort towards a reconciliation of the two standpoints. On July 5th 1415 Huss was summoned before the representatives of the nations in the Minorite monastery, and there Zarabella's formula was submitted to him. But Huss rejected it despite its being, in the sense of the Council, decidedly in his favour. It did not conform to his conscientious scruples. Still, following an order of the Council and King Sigmund, four bishops were sent the same evening to Huss in his prison, where, together with the Bohemian noble Chlum, his companion on his journey to Constance, they tried to persuade him. But Huss retracted nothing. " Wilt thou be wiser than all this congregation ? " asked one of the bishops angrily. " By no means," replied Huss. " I shall gladly accept instruction even from the least among the doctors assembled here, if it only rests on the Gospel."

Huss was then declared an impenitent and, on July 6th, was delivered over to the temporal power for execution.

The Council of Constance aroused considerable

doubt as to its own sanctity.   The life in the small
German town on the Lake of Constance was anything
but holy.   According to the records of the local town
clerk there were at Constance, during the session of
the Council, no less than 700 of so-called " beautiful
ladies," 45 jewellers, 330 merchants, 70 wine sellers,
306 barbers and 346 actors and jugglers.   Yet it is
also true, that among the participants there were some
of the most celebrated lights of the Christian world of
that period, men of pure morals and more erudition
than Huss, to mention only the French Archbishop
Peter d'Ailli and the Chancellor of the Paris university
Gerson, besides some Italians and Englishmen, and it is
noteworthy that it was precisely these best men who
voted for Huss' death.   So preposterous it seemed to
them, in 1415, that an insignificant priest and professor
could oppose the representatives of the whole Church.
To others again it was simply self-evident.   Thus all
that Cardinal Filastre thought of the whole Huss incident in Constance is expressed by his indifferent note :
" In these days the proceedings concerned some Bohemian heretic by the name of Huss and the errors of
Wyclif."

And yet how high morally stood Huss above them
all !   In the course of the last examination one of the
participants was moved to pity for Huss, whom he
recognized as a man of stainless character and noble
mind.   He therefore composed for Huss a retractation
written in words of a general and uncertain meaning,
so that Huss could quiet his conscience because nothing
was actually retracted, and the Council would have the
satisfaction that, after all, Huss did retract.   This
unknown man, whom Huss gratefully calls Pater, also
tried to persuade him, but in vain, as Huss feared for

ever and ever to suffer the reproaches of his conscience
if he should assent to an oath in the least ambiguous.
" If there be any guilt," said the Pater, " it will not
burden thy conscience, but at most that of thy supe-
riors. Not thou wilt condemn the truth, the Council
will do that. Not even the false oath will be charged
to thee, but to those who force thee." This shows
that Huss could have saved his life even at the last
moment, but he was loth to stand before the face of
God as a liar. Here is a proof how the pure teaching
of the Gospel had influence even on higher conceptions
of morality than were represented by the Church, con-
torted, enfeebled and troubled as it was by papal
decrees.

At another time another doctor asked Huss to submit to the Council. This man marvelled at Huss'
courage and said to him, well-meaningly : " Should
the Council declare thou hast only one eye, although
thou hast two, thou must, like the Council, say it is so."
" No," replied Huss. " Even if the whole world
would say that to me, I, having the reason I have now,
could not say such a thing without my conscience
contradicting me." Those were new words in the
Church : the reason and the conscience of the individual as against an authority, violent and omnipotent.
This is the new idea which Huss gave to the world,
that there is no man under the sun who can, by command, force another either to believe or disbelieve
something. The old doctrine of the two swords crum-
bled into dust. The Pope's hand held the teaching,
the Emperor's the compelling sword. But they
neither taught nor compelled Huss to do anything
that was against his reason and conscience.

Was Huss a heretic ? Some historians have tried

to prove (with success) that in Huss' teaching there was no heresy, and that even the Church—being in 1415 not yet clear on certain questions—itself has accepted several of the beliefs for which it condemned Huss. But such proofs are useless, just as the efforts of some patriots, several times repeated, that Huss should be rehabilitated by the Church, as it had always conceded him to have been a pious man. But no, Huss was not only a heretic, but an arch-heretic, as they wrote on the disgraceful cap in which he was led to execution. In his principle, " Here the Church—here the Gospel," were contained all the heresies which either Wyclif or he himself ever did or did not utter. This heresy is the true glory of Huss, of which nobody has a right to rob him.

Huss' is the road of all heretics. Huss wanted to reform the life of Christians, not to alter Church doctrines. But as soon as his opponents, especially the hierarchy, began to attack him, he had to look for support in study and the books of theologians. The first support he found was Wyclif, in his last dispute he appealed to the Gospel and to Christ. The conflict in Constance was between the old and the new world, between the new ideas about the principles and rules of Christian life—the authority lost, the reason and conscience won. This is why Huss is called the torch which threw light into the mediæval darkness. It was a great thing, that personal conviction gained the victory over dictates and interdicts. Personally, Huss lost, but at his stake the mediæval age was also burnt and, following Huss' example, humanity emerged from the mediæval ages. But these liberties were bought with Huss' death !

The first of those whom the stake could not terrify

was the Bohemian nation, which put itself behind Huss almost to a man. The death of an innocent and pure-minded man aroused the common people ; death for an idea and the truth of the Scriptures made irresistible appeal to the intelligentsia. The Bohemian nation became the nation of Huss. Huss gave it a pro-gramme, the foundation of which is the principle of truth and also the principle of progress.

But the smoke of Huss' stake drifted also over foreign countries and wherever it was blown, there, in a few years after Huss' death, Hussites made their appearance—in Germany, in Holland, in Poland and even in England. And a hundred years later Huss won followers in the persons of Luther and Calvin.

This may be the place to show the peculiar character of the Bohemian reformer and to remind the reader in what respects he differs from both Wyclif and Luther. It seems to me that this peculiar character of our heresy is an expression of our national char-acter. Therefore we esteem but lightly the occasional reproach that Huss was not a great theologian. It suffices that he was a great moral character and that he advanced his idea just as well, if not better, than if he had been the most learned theologian in the world.

But what connection is there between all this and the Czech character ? It is difficult and always uncer-tain to find out in what manner some characteristics and striking qualities of the individual nation de-veloped. Why is it that one nation is warlike and the other peaceable ? Why is it that one has commercial talents and the other artistic ? Does the national character grow from the nature of the country in-habited by the nation or will the natural qualities of a nation give character to its country ? Why did we,

Catholic Czechs, have a translation of the Bible already in the fifteenth century, while Catholic Irishmen had not got one up to the middle of the nineteenth ?   Why did the Czechs adhere to the New Testament and the Germans to the old, although the first translator into Visigothic left out, purposely, the bloodthirsty Book of Judges ?

The Czech nation had, from the very dawn of history, much rare ability.   We can see from mediæval literature, that, for example, it always hated rudeness and vulgarity whatever their origin.   At the same time it did not by any means have the " temperament of a dove," which the poetry of eighteenth and nineteenth centuries (Herder's influence) bestowed on it. On the contrary, it was said, " co Čech to hetman " (every Czech is a captain).   And the older historians were full of admiration of the chivalry of the old Czechs, it being unheard of that a Czech broke his given word, suffered his honour to be insulted or bore in silence any wrong done to others.   Yet how does the fact compare with all this, that our nation from time immemorial also loved music and song and was possessed of great artistic talents ?   On this point both the foreign and native thinkers agree that our nation is endowed with sensibility and imagination. These two qualities, though not indicating mobility or instability of mind, are little open to abstract thinking.   For a nature of that sort loves pictures, wants to see objects rather than to think of them.   You will hardly get a Czech to speculate philosophically on generalities.   After all, we have some predilection for philosophy too (for a part of religion—doctrine—is always philosophical), but, above all, we love that which is illustrative, vivid and almost palpable.

It was, therefore, not a mere accident that even those who in the fourteenth and fifteenth centuries became absorbed in thought about religion were not allured by the subtleties of philosophy, but rather by its other aspect, the morality and the doctrine of practical life. Thus began Milič and Štítný, and Huss followed in their footsteps. Thus it is no accident that their heir Komenský (Comenius) became a pioneer of the intuitive method of instruction, which forms an epoch in pedagogic history. In the fifteenth century moral philosophy was a palpable matter, easy of comprehension and directly utilizable ; in the seventeenth century Komenský saw the means for the reform of humanity in a good school, and that, if the school is to produce a noble-minded generation, educational methods must be improved.

Nevertheless, the moral side of religion cannot be separated long from doctrine, for the reason that the basis of every good practice is a good theory. Therefore Milič fell, *nolens volens*, into heresy, and Huss died in it. He became the greatest heretic of the Middle Ages, an arch-heretic. But Huss could not be wholly explained as a heretic by the sensibility and imaginativeness of his character if the Czech character were not possessed of another distinct quality.

This is tenacity in adhering to a recognized truth, for once a Czech sets his teeth into a matter that is clear to him, nobody will ever tear him away from it. And Huss' idea was of this kind. It was obvious, therefore, even to the dullest comprehension, that Huss strove to bring into life something beautiful, pure and desirable—human love in the spirit of Christ's teachings—in order to rid the world of evil, or at least that the evil be lessened. In this he persisted even to the

E

stake and for that also died the Hussite people, being
deeply convinced that they were " warriors of God."

Here are a few indications of the character of the
Czechs of that period :

One day a feeble old man crept into Huss' prison
and began to relate, in a hypocritical and meek manner,
that he was an ordinary monk, poor and ignorant, and
that having heard so much laudable of Huss, he would
like to have his opinion of the Holy Communion.
When Huss answered him in good faith, and the old
man appeared dismayed and repeated his question to
Huss three times over, John of Chlum, who was present,
rebuked him sharply, saying it was not good manners
to doubt the word of an honest man.   After the monk
left, Huss learned that his tempter was no other than
Fra Didacus, a famous Spanish theologian, the same
who later evinced so much joy that Huss was burnt (in
his letter to the King of Spain, July 8th 1415).

This same John of Chlum was also present when
Huss was examined.   Peter d'Ailli asked Huss,
whether it be true what he said after his incarceration,
namely, that he came to Constance of his own free will
and that if he had been unwilling to come neither the
King of Bohemia nor of Rome could have compelled
him to do so.   Huss replied that he did express himself to that effect and that there were many Bohemian
lords who loved him and who had given him an asylum
in their castles.   The judges showing their displeasure
at this, Chlum said in support of Huss' words : " I am
but a poor knight in our country, yet I would defend
him for a whole year, whether anybody liked it or not,
so that no one should get him.   And there are many
more powerful, who would defend him as long as
they wished, even against both of those kings."

This knight of Chlum showed himself, while in Constance, once more to be a Czech character. When, on July 5th, four bishops tried to persuade Huss, Chlum joined them, saying : " Thou seest, magister, we are only laymen and cannot advise thee in these matters. If thou feelest thou art guilty of anything, be not ashamed to be instructed and to retract. However, if thy conscience tells thee thou art not guilty of the things they charge thee with, do nothing against thy conscience, lie not before the face of God, but rather persevere in the truth thou hast acknowledged."

The character of Chlum shows how effectively men like Milič and Huss could arouse the conscience of their countrymen. Milič and Huss were both as pious as they were honourable and chivalrous. Most assuredly, the knight of Chlum was not alone in this respect, as the near future abundantly showed.

Hussitism, in its true form, was born in Bohemia after the death of Huss and Jerome, the latter being burnt later, also in Constance. This Hussitism developed, five years after Huss' death, into a national programme. While Huss' idea was purely religious, five years after his death Hussitism means much more. Friedrich Bezold expresses it briefly as follows : " All that we include in the name of Hussitism, is a conglomeration and combination of religious, national and social-political ideas."

The Council of Constance had to occupy itself with Bohemian affairs even after the death of both martyrs at the beginning of September 1415. The general diet of the Bohemian and Moravian Estates assembled in Prague and at once forwarded a sharp protest against the burning of Huss to the holy fathers. There were 452 seals hanging from the protest roll.

As against these Hussites, only fourteen nobles met in Český Brod to issue from there a statement that, according to the customs of their ancestors, they would obey the King, the Church and the Council of Constance. Great joy was felt in the latter town, because this new league was joined, in person, by the King himself. The Council replied to the protest by sending home the Bishop of Litomyšl, John Železný, with an order to annihilate Huss' followers with both the spiritual and temporal sword. But the bishop found at home such conditions that he scarcely dared to show himself in public. All he did was to place Prague under an interdict because Magister John of Jesenice was allowed to stay there unmolested, although he had been for several years past under papal interdict. Then in February 1416, the Council ordered all the 452 Bohemian lords and knights who sent the threatening letter to Constance, to appear before its tribunal, and made all the necessary preparation for their trial, namely, hung out the legal notices of it at Passau, Vienna and Ratisbon. The Archbishop of Prague and the Bishop of Olomouc escaped a similar prosecution by the Council only because King Sigmund thought that things had gone far enough as it was.

From time to time complaints were also heard in Constance against King Václav and Queen Sophia, reproaching the King with taking no steps against the Hussites and the Queen with being ever the protectress of John of Jesenice as she had been formerly of Huss. Václav IV took the Constance threats but lightly, defended the Bishop of Olomouc, who was deposed by the Church Council, against that body, and did not allow the new Council's nominee, John Železný, even to enter the country.

In the meantime the Council was receiving tidings of the agitation and religious troubles taking place both at Prague and in the country. It therefore hurled interdicts against Bohemia, especially against the priests who served the Holy Communion in both kinds, against the Prague University (which was deprived of all its special statutory privileges) because it had justified the use of the chalice at the Lord's Supper and of the Scriptures. But finally the learned chancellor of the Paris University declared that it would be better to make war on the Bohemians with the sword rather than with mere words.

There was no change in the sentiment of the Church Council when Pope Martin V was elected. On the contrary, this Pope confirmed all the measures taken by the Council against the Bohemians, but as a last resource called upon the Bohemians and Moravians to return to the obedience of the Church, placed the disobedient and intractable under an interdict, and ordered both the spiritual and temporal authorities to resort to legal punishment when necessary. He would also have proceeded with the action against King Václav and the League of 452 members of the Estates, if King Sigmund had not restrained him in the hope that his brother would come to his senses on realizing the danger by which his throne was threatened. It should be added in explanation, that King Václav IV gave, even as late as June 9th 1418, to all the messages sent him by the Council and his brother Sigmund, an answer as gruff as eloquent. For he had a law proclaimed that no Bohemian of secular state should appear before any Church tribunal beyond the frontiers. This law served by way of welcome to Cardinal John Dominici, whom the Council sent, in July 1418, to Bohemia to weed out heresy there.

King Sigmund was returning at the end of the summer of 1418 from the German Empire to his Hungarian Kingdom, bringing Cardinal Dominici with him. From Passau he sent an impressive admonition to his brother in Bohemia. But not to his brother alone—his letter was scattered in many copies all over Bohemia, so that his brother might be also warned by others. The letter stated that Václav's forbearance and indecision would inevitably lead to horrible consequences, as the nations of all Christian countries were on the verge of rising against the King should he continue to favour the heretics, and that King Sigmund had, in the meantime, diverted the interdict which had several times already been prepared against both the country and the nation, because he trusted his brother's promises, but that he would intercede no more, as by doing so he would bring the suspicion upon himself that he esteemed blood-relationship above the Christian faith. If then—the warning continued—the whole of Christendom should rise against the Bohemians, depose King Václav and free his subjects from their oath of fidelity to their King—he, Sigmund, washed his hands of this misfortune and would bring to justice all those who, by their disobedience, should compel him to take such step. A little later, from Linz, Sigmund called upon Václav to send, on February 9th 1419, a number of nobles, whom he named himself, to a meeting at Uherská Skalice, for a last conference on how to weed out the heretics in the Bohemian nation.

These threats did not fail to cause King Václav to waver, and in fact he began to hinder the Hussites in several ways. Having banished Magister Jesenice from

Prague, he ordered the Catholic priests in Prague to be reinstated to the posts they had been ejected from, although to the Hussites he still left three churches and two monasteries in the town. By this he secured, on February 26th 1419, the annulment of the interdict against Prague, and church services began to be held again.

It was, however, already too late for peace and religious order in the country. Both in Bohemia and Moravia a new world began to awaken, which cared little or nothing at all for either the threats of the Council or papal interdicts. The Catholic chronicler of that time makes the reproach against the King that it was then much too late to stop the fire, as he had " allowed the spark to become red-hot coals."

The Bohemian people was greatly agitated by the burning of pure-minded and learned men, of pious preachers and speakers. It could not understand the cruelty with which they were treated nor their death, when, at the same time, it read in Huss' letters and also heard from witnesses arrived from Constance, that the holy congregation there led a life of loose morals that gave offence to all decent people. These observations deprived the Bohemians of all respect for a body claiming to be the highest representation of Christianity, and what followed after the years 1415 and 1416 could not improve in the least the opinion that the common people had formed of Constance, that Huss and Jerome were national saints, the Pope and the Church Council mere tools of Antichrist.

The people thronged to the sermons of Huss' followers and Catholic priests were driven from their parishes. Other adherents of Huss again went through the country gathering believers around them. The learned magisters of Prague University debated on the theological consequences of Huss' teaching. We know of a few early country centres of the Hussite movement, as, for instance, at Ústí Sezimově on the Lužnice, in Pilsen and the neighbourhood, around Knin, in the Šumava towns and elsewhere. Ústí was the most alive of them all, probably because of the seed sown there abundantly by Huss, who preached and wrote at Kozí Hrádek near by. Thus in Prague Hussitism was under the leadership of men of learning, in the country it was a movement of the people. The first was a conservative element, the second a radical. Both, however, were permeated in common by the desire for the reform of the Christian life. Their mutual symbol was the chalice, i.e. the communion in both kinds, as it was introduced in Prague by Magister Jakoubek of Stříbro, already before Huss' death and with his approval.

How rapidly Bohemian Hussitism and the resistance to Rome spread among the nations of all Europe is testified by several unusual occurrences. In 1413 there arrived in Prague Peter Payne, a master of arts of Oxford University and a prominent disciple of Wyclif. Being accepted by the Bohemian University professors, he eloquently propagated his teacher's doctrines. The Bohemians called him " Mr. English." There also came, in 1418, about forty Frenchmen who settled permanently in Prague. These again were Waldensians, led by their own minister. The Prague people received them hospitably, and even Queen Sophia went to visit them occasionally. Their minister read to them in French, but they never took part in the Hussite service. While English, as a Wyclifist, undoubtedly was the cause of the warning which the Prague University issued to the people that it should keep off all innovations except those recommended by the magisters of Prague, in the south the religious movement showed itself in a way that was hard to control. The people went up to the mountains. On the mountains divine services were held as well as conferences, the meaning of which was then not yet understood.

The year 1419 marks the beginning of domestic revolts and also of the Hussite wars.

The indications of the coming storms appeared in the country in those great gatherings of people on the mountains. The order for them was given by the Hussite priests, who were ejected by the Catholic majority from Ústí Sezimové. They met with their followers in the open air on the top of an extensive hill near Bechyně. They gave the hill the Biblical name of Mount Tábor. There the priests preached and administered to the people the Lord's Supper in both kinds. Such a gathering was held there on July 22nd 1419, to which invitations were sent all over Bohemia and Moravia and which drew there more than 40,000 people, who came, according to old custom, with standards flying and singing hymns. Again there was nothing else but preaching, confession, communion and in the afternoon a common feast and religious debate after the Biblical example of the Sermon on the Mount, yet it was also a demonstration against the wavering King Václav. The King supposed Nicholas of Husi, a former governor of his castle at Husinec, to be one of the organizers of his great pilgrimage and gave a willing ear to the insinuations that Nicholas would like to depose him from the throne in order to occupy it himself.

What contemporary evidence has been preserved to us regarding the spirit of this meeting on Mount Tábor, is highly significant. All the participants began to call one another brother and sister ; their common meal from what the pilgrims had brought individually signified that there was no difference between mine and thine, and that it thus should remain so in the future. Music, dance and worldly songs were banned. Nor were complaints about the persecution of those faithful to the word of God lacking.

But if the gatherings on the mountains were mere signals of the threatening storm, the storm itself actually broke loose, in Prague, in 1419. Among the various measures taken by King Václav against the Hussites was that of filling the Prague New Town Council entirely with men known for their enmity to Huss' teachings. These new councillors—as bold as they were blind to the conditions around them—were guilty of various rash acts. For example, they persuaded the King to deprive the Hussites of all their schools in the New Town and themselves brutally maltreated a Hussite procession. The preacher in the Church of St. Mary of the Snow, John called Želivský (from his former connection with the Želiv monastery), a man of stormy temper and much daring, had a dominating influence over the lower classes of the Prague population. On July 30th he led a procession from his own church to the Church of St. Stephen. When the returning procession was passing the New Town Hall, Želivský stopped and sent the councillors a message demanding the discharge from prison of some Hussites who shortly before had been arrested for adhering to the doctrine of the chalice. This the councillors refused to do and one of them even threw a stone from a window at the sacrament which the priest John was carrying.

This was the last straw. The excited multitude attacked and broke into the Town Hall, and then " a murder, enormous and unheard-of, was committed in the New Town at Prague "—as the old chronicler records—" by the burghers and other mad people of that town, so that they killed thirteen councillors and the mayor Niklásek, throwing them down from the windows of the Town Hall which they, at the 14th hour before dinner, then occupied by force. And such cruelties have they done to them forcing them to fall on spears and halberds and on swords and daggers. And he who was not stabbed thus they instantly beat to death, but at that moment they did not take from them what they wore, only laying their caps and their silver belts on their bodies. And after this murder the Old Town councillors came to an agreement with them, fearing lest the same might happen to them as to the New Towners."

When, during the attack on the New Town Hall, the bells in Prague began to ring in alarm, the King's under-chamberlain hurried to the assistance of the councillors with 300 horsemen, but, seeing the immense throng opposing him, judiciously declined to interfere. The victors immediately appointed in the captured Town Hall four town captains for their defence. The captains then summoned the burghers by threats to appear before them. But nobody dared attack.

King Václav IV was staying at that time at Nový Hrádek near Kunratice. Learning of the trouble, he swore high and low that he would punish the rioters, especially the priests, with the utmost severity, and

root out the whole Hussite sect.   His paroxysm was
so violent that it brought on a fit of apoplexy causing
paralysis all over his left side.   He died there August
16th 1419, apparently in great pain, for the old
chronicler recorded that he " died . . . uttering loud
cries and roarings as if a lion's."

*   *   *   *   *

It may be asked what the name, Huss, signifies for
the Bohemians of to-day.   In our opinion, his importance is not merely national, but world-wide.   The
learned Bohemians, in explaining the details of his
heresy, always arrive at the same conclusion.   There
was a time (in 1869) when a Bohemian newspaper
voiced the opinion that the process against Huss should
be revised and the accusation of heresy be withdrawn,
as his deviations from the official doctrine were of the
slightest.   But even if we overlook the expression of
the papal journal of those days : " Fools !   Great
fools ! " the opinion quoted above was in itself incor-
rect.   For the Huss who rejected the old system of
Rome's authority over the souls of men, was an arch-
heretic, and the glory of that name will always abide
with him.   From the historical standpoint the disputes about Huss' teachings are very interesting and
the average intelligent Czech public looks at the matter
as settled for good.   Whether Huss did realize the
consequences of his resistance or not, he succeeded in
liberating the reason of the individual and granted
the Christian the right to base his relations to God on
his own judgment and conscience.   Huss' struggle
with Rome was, moreover, accompanied by a wonderful firmness of character and great moral purity.
This the nation acknowledged and resolved to follow

Huss in these virtues. Likewise, Huss' steadfastness in the doctrine based on conviction and those virtues of his life, which nobody ever could or ever will be able to diminish, are a precious heritage and the glory of all modern society. The Bohemian nation took up as an inheritance from Huss the fight for truth, respect for personal conviction, loyalty to freedom and a love of fraternity and democracy none of which it ever betrayed until conquered and demoralized by the counter-reformation. Fortunately for itself, the Bohemian nation began, soon after its renaissance, to return to these ideals. And the nations which have surpassed the Bohemians in development—and even of this did Huss lay the foundations—recognized in 1918, that Huss' nation is entitled to liberty, the gates of which Huss was opening already in the beginning of the fifteenth century.

There is, therefore, full justification for speaking of Huss' world significance. Even foreign authors recall it by pointing to the road over which Huss' idea travelled to Luther, from Luther to the era of enlightenment and finally to the Declaration of Human Rights on both shores of the Atlantic Ocean (in Virginia in 1776 and in Paris in 1793). The sense of these rights is, that what Huss claimed for the individual, the Declaration grants to whole nations.

Mazzini spoke of " a holy man, John Huss of Bohemia, who perished in the flames of the Inquisition." To the readers of his time he gave the following explanation. " Nowadays the majority of you do not know the history of those struggles or you consider them to have been the struggles of fanatics, on questions purely theological. But once history becomes popular through national education and shows you

that any progress in religious questions is immediately
followed by a corresponding progress in civil life,
then you will understand the true worth of those quarrels and will also honour the memory of its martyrs as
that of your benefactors." To Mazzini the Great
Revolution was the work of Protestantism. At first
the individual had to struggle for his own rights ; in
modern times he desires to co-operate with his nation.

Louis Blanc, in his *History of the French Revolution*,
gave its first book the title " Jean Hus." From him
the evolution stretches into the eighteenth century.
To let people drink from the chalice signified an act of
equality. The Bohemians, in desiring to be free,
desired to be brothers.

A similar idea was expressed by a Russian, Alexander
Herzen. On seeing the Paris revolution of 1848
frustrated, he exclaimed : " Where are the holy
standards which gained to Huss admirers in one camp
and the year 1789 in a second ? "

III

John Žižka and the Hussite Warfare

IN the Hussite movement Žižka's name appears as
early as the time when Magister John Huss used
to preach in the Bethlehem chapel.   In the Brotherhood memoirs (published later, of course) we find a
note, that Huss " was aided by King Václav," and that
" the Queen, with her chamberlain John Žižka, used to
attend his sermons."

Martin Luther's Bohemian Chronicle of 1539 (thus
also a later one) records that John Žižka served at
King Václav's court even after Huss was burnt.   It
is said that one day the King, seeing Žižka sad, which
was contrary to his usual manner, asked him the reason
of it.   Žižka answered : " Most gracious King, how
could I be merry, when our faithful leaders and true
teachers of the law of God are being burnt to death
by the false priests ? "   To which the King said :
"Dear John, what can we say now, can we mend it
at all ?   If thou knowest a way, mend it for thyself ;
we wish thee well in it."   And Žižka is said to have
taken the King at his word, replying that with his permission he would do so.

How long Žižka remained in the King's service, we
do not know.   The second time his name appears in
public was on July 30th 1419, in connection with the

storming of the New Town Hall. Two trustworthy contemporary witnesses state that Žižka took a prominent part in storming the Town Hall. His biographer, V. V. Tomek, is of the opinion that at that time Žižka was still a member of the King's retinue, serving in the Vyšehrad garrison when Queen Sophia and her co-regent Čeněk of Vartenberk began to become reconciled to the succession of King Sigmund to the Bohemian throne.

After King Václav's death the events in the country were tending towards war. The meetings of the people in the rural districts continued. For September 30th 1419 a great meeting was announced at a place called " Na křížkách," which caused serious uneasiness, partly on account of its proximity to Prague, and partly because the invitation stated that the object of the gathering was " the unity in God *for the freedom of the law of God*," and also because examples of the heroism of the people of Israel were cited. But in Prague itself, already on August 17th, when the death of the King became known, the hatred, accumulated in the people against the anti-Huss priests and monks for all the wrongs done to the Hussites in the last few months, broke loose. The maddened crowds threw themselves on some of the churches and monasteries, which they pillaged, destroying the altars, paintings of saints, organs, sacred utensils and so forth. In the evening the rioting increased, and the stately Carthusian monastery at what is now Smíchov was ransacked and then given over to the flames, its monks being taken to Prague. The following day more churches and also the houses of Catholic burghers were pillaged. On the third day the dwellings of the prostitutes were destroyed all over the city.

ŽIŽKA.

[*To face p.* 80

From Prague the anti-clerical storms passed over to other towns—to Písek, Klatovy, Plzeň, Hrad Louny and Žatec.

These excesses filled the Bohemian Estates with dread, and the nobility therefore insisted that an orderly administration be established in the country as soon as possible. No doubt existed that according to the laws of the country, the King of Germany and Hungary, Sigmund, was the heir to the vacant throne. Nevertheless, the Estates saw themselves compelled to stipulate some conditions, knowing him to be an old enemy of Hussitism. But the King put them off with meaningless words.

Although the meeting of the people " Na křížkách " ended peacefully—it was attended by pilgrims even from Prague—yet before it separated the fiery preacher of Plzen, Václav Koranda, appealed to all to come to the next great meeting on November 10th in Prague, not with pilgrim's staffs, but with swords in their hands. For though " the vineyard of God blossomed out well, he-goats are also approaching, desiring to gnaw the vine off." A great part of these pilgrims entered Prague late at night, by way of Vyšehrad, accompanying the Prague brothers and sisters to their homes. Prague received them hospitably. Unfortunately, they joined for several days in excesses against the churches and monasteries, such as had taken place after the death of King Václav. By this they terrorized Prague to such a degree that the city gladly joined, on October 6th, the armed league headed by Queen Sophia and the nobility.

The Old Chronicler records expressly the date of the beginning of the war. On September 30th it had not yet begun. He says about the passage of the

F

pilgrims through Vyšehrad : " Some may wonder that being strong enough to take Vyšehrad they have not done so ; for near this very castle much evil and cruelty happened to the Prague people in the same year, and with great labour and expense as well as bloodshed they had to lay siege to it afterwards. . . . I believe that it happened thus because they did not occupy it right at the start, *as then the real war had not yet begun.*"

After the Prague riots, in which the radical town element were joined by the pilgrims, negotiations were begun between the magisters of Prague and the Táborite priests.   They ended in a resolution in regard to certain principles, on which both sides were of the same mind.   This resolution forms the basis of the Hussite creed, i.e. the famous *four Prague articles*, stipulating :

1. That the Word of God be preached by capable priests in the sense of the Redeemer freely and without hindrance.

2. That all mortal, especially the public, sins and other vices hateful to God, irrespective of the class they be committed by, should in a proper, judicious and Christian manner, and by those whose duty it is, be forbidden, prosecuted, punished and, as far as possible, rooted out.

3. That the Lord's Supper in both kinds, bread and wine, be administered free to all Christians, excepting those guilty of mortal sin, and be received by them.

4. That the clergy, giving up temporal rule over property and worldly goods, which they hold to the detriment of their office and of the temporal arm, live according to the teaching of Christ and his apostles, which is frugally and temperately.

The war began before long, and in connection with the people's camp meetings. That is to say, as the anniversary of St. Ludmila (November 10th) approached, pilgrims gathered on all sides and in great numbers to go to Prague on that day. And the Old Chronicler relates : " Then it came to pass, that such lords who were already in the pay of King Sigmund of Hungary, and by whom the castles and many towns in the Kingdom of Bohemia were occupied, hindered, with all their might, the people from assembling and going ; and on account of that great wars did begin."

But they were begun by the King's men, not by the people. The King's burgraves received orders not to allow the people's meetings and the Catholic nobles acted without orders. The first collision was on November 4th, when Count Peter Konopištský of Sternberg, at the head of 1,300 riders, both his own and numbers from the town of Kutná Hora, killed many pilgrims from Sezimovo Ústí and made about 100 of them prisoners. These were pilgrims who were going to Prague in procession and had agreed with the pilgrims from Knín and with others from Western Bohemia to rendezvous on the River Vltava near Knín. But the slaughter did not stop there— those who had been taken prisoners met the same fate, for the fierce miners in Kutná Hora, mostly of German nationality, were the greatest enemies the Hussites had. Kutná Hora, with its abundance of silver, was at that period the next largest Bohemian town to Prague, of which it was inordinately jealous. The prisoners taken at Sezimovo Ústí were first tortured and then, while still alive, cast into the deepest shafts. These were the first Hussite martyrs. Later Kutná Hora gained great notoriety by persecution of this kind.

According to the Old Chronicler : " The bishop of Litomyšl, with the Lord Peter Konopištský, with the miners and other lords, conspired in order to destroy all those who received the Holy Communion in both kinds. And thus many poor people started to capture priests whom they then brought to Hora (mountain—Kutná Hora, mining mountain). For every man thus delivered in Hora they received one sack of groats and for a priest five sacks. And they also caught herdsmen in the fields and sold people in Hora as they would cattle."

When the report reached Prague on November 4th of what had befallen the Ústí pilgrims, the town bells started ringing an alarm, calling the people together with a view to sending help. But, contrary to all expectations, the people thus assembled did not leave Prague. On the contrary, they threw themselves upon Malá Strana,[1] which was then occupied by the royalists, took the greater part of that part of the town and came near taking the Castle too, from which Queen Sophia fled in fear of her life. In these fights John Žižka became so prominent that he was taken by the people at his word. " From this time on Žižka's fame continued to grow to the end of his life."

Žižka, who thus came into prominence, was a country squire from the village of Trocnov in Southern Bohemia, south-east of Budějovice, a village which now no longer exists. In this village there were two freeholds and a handful of people subject to the squires. One of the freeholds was owned by Ješek (John) of Trocnov, to whom, at the end of the reign of Charles IV, a son, John, was born. This is our John Žižka. The father, John, the mother, Catherine.

[1] The part of Prague on the left bank of the Vltava.

Old records mention, besides, an aunt, Anne; a sister, Agnes ; and a brother, Jaroslav. And we also know that our Žižka was a widower and that his daughter was married to a knight, Ondřej of Dubé. This is all we know of his family. We would gladly ask those old chroniclers for more, for some more intimate details, but their documents refuse to answer. We would ask if it be true that the word Žižka was a nick-name of the red-headed ; we would ask where Žižka lost his first eye ; how old he was in 1419 when he began to fight, of what stature he was and what were his features—but in vain. The sources give no answer.

According to an old story, Žižka was born under an oak, where his mother sought shelter in a thunderstorm which drove her from the field. When John reached his early manhood, quarrels broke out between King Václav IV and the nobility, of which latter the Lord of Rožmberk was the most powerful. The Rožm-berks were " the kings of South Bohemia." The small nobles held with the King against the great lords ; and so did the knights of Trocnov. In 1407 we find John Žižka and his brother Jaroslav among the declared enemies not only of the Rožmberks but also of the arrogant and selfish town of Budějovice. In the Rožmberk Executioner's journal Žižka was marked down as a " robber," for he and his com-panions, of both squire and peasant families, attacked their enemies' farms and drove away their cattle, held up merchants on the highways and took their goods, hiding then either in the woods or in the villages, where the peasants always knew how to conceal them. They also had protectors in the families of some of the higher nobility who stood by the King. This guerilla warfare was ended by King Václav IV in 1409, by his simply requesting the town of Budějovice to come to an agreement with Žižka, and a little later " he received in grace John called Žižka, his dear faithful one," at the same time ordering the Budějovice people also to recognize him as " good." In all probability the King prevailed upon Jindřich of Rožmberk to do likewise.

After that, Žižka appeared on battlefields that lay far from his country—in Poland and Lithuania. In 1410 he fought on the side of the Poles and Lithuanians against the order of the Teutonic Knights, in company with other experienced warriors, whose prowess was greatly lauded by the Polish chronicler, Canon Dlugoš, who, although later a fierce hater of the Hussites, says of John Žižka explicitly, that the King of Poland liked him very much, as he was, despite his youth, already a warrior of experience.

Following this the reports we have of Žižka are but poor. We even do not know the date of his enrolment among the " servants (familiaris domini regis) " of King Václav's court in Prague. The old records only say that at one time he was the gate-keeper at the royal court and at one time the chamberlain of Queen Sophia, whom he often accompanied to hear Huss' sermons.

At the time Žižka was taken by the people " at his word," that is, in 1419, he already had only one eye. And as there appears to have been, amongst the lesser court officers, also a certain page Janek (Jack) the one-eyed, it is probable that this One-eyed Jack is Žižka himself. Should that be the case, then we have learned one more detail concerning Žižka, which is, that he bought, in 1414, a house " na Příkopě " (on the Moat) for fifty sacks of groats. This would about correspond with the wealth of the squire of Trocnov.

After the taking of the Malá Strana there followed, through four years of Žižka's life, a long chain of campaigns over Bohemia, Moravia and Slovakia, which are marked out by both larger and smaller victories ; their number, and the dangerous conditions under which they were secured, almost taking one's breath away. These victorious battles were also the foundation of Žižka's fame as that of a genial and invincible warrior.

It was in the country that the long chain of Žižka's splendid victories was begun. Together with the knight Břeněk Švihovský of Skála and the knight Chval Řepický of Machovice who, on November 6th 1419, had conducted the Plzeň and Ústí pilgrims to Prague, Žižka then left the city and marching on Plzeň, took possession of it. In this troop Žižka was already accepted as the commander-in-chief, and commander-in-chief of the Hussite and Táborite armies he remained to his death.

There, in the Plzeň territory, the chief opponent of the Hussites was Bohuslav of Švamberk, who with his army attempted to reconquer Plzeň for King Sigmund. Žižka, however, not only succeeded in holding the town, but even made sorties into the neighbourhood. Some time in December 1419 he attacked the fort of Nekměř north of Plzeň and took it, but on his way back to Plzeň was intercepted by Bohuslav of Švamberk. Žižka easily defeated him, and the same night, before returning to Plzeň, he demolished three forts in the neighbourhood. At this battle of Nekměř we learn, for the first time, something of the strategical organization of Žižka's army. He marched on Nekměř with 300 infantry and 7 wagons, in which he carried guns for breaking down walls. Švamberk had over 2,000 of both mounted men and infantry. His cavalry attacked Žižka fiercely, but Žižka used his wagons as a bastion for his infantry and both frustrated and repulsed the attack.

From Žižka's second battle with a superior number of enemy we already learn more of his army. This was at Sudoměř.

The former South Bohemian pilgrims to Mount Tábor had developed into armed troops. One detachment of them, directed by a scholar or sexton, Hromádka of Jistebnice, took, on February 21st 1420, the town of Sezimovo Ústí by force. But the town not being strong enough, he left it with his troops in a few days and possessed himself of the stout castle of Hradiště on the Lužnice, below which then lay, in ruins, the town of Hradiště, demolished a century and a half before. There Hromádka settled down ; the pilgrims began to repair the old houses and to build huts hurriedly. This new site received the name of Tábor. Hromádka sent information about all this to Žižka in Plzeň, asking at the same time for reinforcements. Žižka sent him a part of his army under the command of Chval of Machovice. In the meantime a strong royal army was beleaguering Žižka in Plzeň, and there was still another army being collected against him. Then, when Žižka weakened himself by sending help to Tábor, the Catholic party in Plzeň also took courage, and thus Žižka found it advisable to conclude an armistice and give up the town on honourable terms.

He next proceeded to Tábor, taking with him the Hussite families who no longer felt safe enough in

Plzeň ; his whole force did not consist of more than 400 men, 12 wagons and 9 riding horses. On this march Žižka had no desire to meet the royal army, which was then marching from Kutná Hora and Benešov by way of Písek to Plzeň, although an armistice had been made by the royalist party. Being informed by their spies what direction Žižka had taken, they intercepted him, one party marching against him from the east, the other (Švamberk's) from the west. And despite its being St. Mary's Day (March 25th), the nobles assailed Žižka near the village of Sudoměř. This battle aroused amazement throughout the whole country, even the Hussite descendants afterwards talking about it with bated breath, as we learn from the records of the Old Chronicler : " When Žižka passed through Štěkeň and was marching on towards Sudoměř, at that time the King's men, very strong in numbers, arrived at Písek on their expedition against Žižka in the Plzeň country. And when they learned on the way from their scouts, that Žižka was making towards Sudoměř, all these troops went at once after him. And from the other side again marched Jindřich, the knight of the Cross of Strakonice, with many from the Pilzeň country, so that too great a multitude had assembled against a few people. At that time Žižka had just left Sudoměř, in the direction of a fish-pond called ' The Ugly,' and then, unable to go any farther, he set up his defence, backing his wagons up to the dam, and there with his few people he manfully resisted that great multitude, for the enemy surrounded him on every side, since the pond had then been emptied and was without water. And many people have said since then that even had they not beaten them with anything at all, but simply pressed them with their horses, the horses' hoofs had surely crushed them there and then. But because the Lord God was with him (there and elsewhere, for Žižka was a true servant of His), therefore a wonder never seen before happened. Although it was still early, about the vesper hour, the sun was seen to sink behind the hill as if he wanted to part from them and it grew dark at once, so that nobody could distinguish whom to strike. At that moment the knight Břeněk, aid to Brother Žižka, was killed and on the King's side many were killed and wounded. Certain it is, that Žižka's men slew more than the enemy did. When this wonder was observed by the enemy, they spoke with many voices : My spear will not strike, my sword will not cut, my cross-bow will not shoot them ! And so they marched away separately, to their great shame and having suffered much injury. Žižka remained on the battlefield all night ; then at dawn, putting his men and his wagons, which suffered no damage, in marching order, he proceeded to Castle Újezdec, where he encamped till sent for by the Tábor people, and there he was received gloriously and with great honours."

It was about March 27th or 28th when Žižka entered Tábor. His idea was to concentrate in this new town as big a force as possible. Therefore he also brought the rest of the population from Ústí to Tábor, and the now deserted town was, on March 30th, given over to the flames. The fortifications of Tábor and the inner tangle of its streets, both of which can be still recognized, excite the admiration even of modern strategists, native as well as foreign. And while houses and bastions were being built in the town with all speed, Žižka launched military attacks in the neighbourhood. One of them is memorable. The Master of the Mint, Divůček, with about 1,000 of "iron lords," was, after the battle of Sudoměř, resting in the castle and little town of Vožice. On Good Friday, April 5th, Žižka approached Vožice by night, attacked and defeated Divůček and possessed himself of both the horses and armour of the riders, using it in forming a cavalry for himself. Other reports tell us that first of all he trained the troops which came with him from the Plzeň country in the use of wagons in battle.

The army thus formed by Žižka was essentially a peasant army. The peasants and country-squires from Central Bohemia moved, with their wives and children, to the new town of Tábor. The peasants formed the kernel of the army, the squire class furnished the leaders. Of course, this human material could be armed only with such weapons as it could use, thus the farm tools had to be transformed into weapons of war. There were flails with nails driven into them, halberds forged from pitch-forks by the blacksmiths, and long hooks used by the peasants for pulling the riders from their saddles. And there were the peasant wagons, which had to become a rampart protecting the soldiers during the fight, on the march, and, finally, when attacking. This wagon bulwark was the great surprise of that time. Surprising, of course, was the fact alone that Žižka could create out of the common people, mostly of the peasant class, a good army, against which trained troops, whether the King's or the nobility's, were impotent. Forced marches and an ingenuous utilization of the ground also formed an important part of Žižka's tactics.

This army was put under such discipline as was

hitherto unheard of in the history of war. This indeed was a necessity for an army of peasants, entirely without military training. Žižka's army began battles with prayers and a religious chant, during which the troops knelt. Into this song was inserted, after four religious verses, the military regulations, which were thus impressed on the memory of the soldiers before every battle. There was in particular the famous battle hymn : " *Ye who are the Warriors of God.*" The army declared itself in this song to be " God's warriors " and kept up its spirit by trusting in God, for whom it is necessary to sacrifice temporal life in return for eternal life. And then follow the principles : (1) " Ye who are the warriors of God, consider not the numbers of the enemy and never run from him. (2) Risk not your lives, ye warriors of God, for avarice or loot. (3) Ye warriors of God, neglect not the fight for the gathering of booty. (4) Ye warriors of God, remember the army parole ; obey your captains, observe their movements and hold fast to your troop. (5) God's warriors must help each other. (6) The warriors of God begin their attack with a rousing cry : " Hr (hurrah) at them ! "

This hymn was not composed by Žižka himself, but whoever did compose it must have been well acquainted with his spirit as well as his intentions, ideas and principles.

In the spring of 1420 Žižka proceeded with the arming of the Bohemian people and the preaching of a holy war. Expedition was necessary, as Pope Martin V, in concert with King Sigmund, had declared a crusade of the whole Christian world against the Bohemians. King Sigmund was then at Vratislav (Breslau) and there came to him there the German

princes as well as volunteers from all European countries. But he also had many adherents in the Bohemian nobility, for the situation was different from that
in 1415 when, in the general Bohemian diet, 452
nobles, who had formed themselves into a league, protested against the actions of the Council of Constance,
while only fourteen nobles joined the Catholic League
then in session at Český Brod. For as soon as King
Sigmund proclaimed himself heir to the Bohemian
throne, the nobility at once began to acknowledge him
as their future master. However, Sigmund's hatred
of the chalice exasperated the Bohemian people, and
especially the people of Prague and of some other towns,
especially after Sigmund had had dragged to death
by horses in Breslau, the prominent Prague merchant
Krása, who came there to attend the annual fair, and
then had the horribly tortured man burnt at the stake
(March 15th). Thus only Žižka and the people of
Prague prepared to defend the country against the
undesirable King. But at that moment the country's
administrator, Čeněk of Vartenberk, also became dis-
gusted, " as a Czech and Hussite," with the King for
his cruelty at Breslau. He made an agreement with
the people of Prague, and issued a proclamation to all
the Czechs and Moravians to the effect that Sigmund,
the King of Germany and Hungary, had shown himself an enemy of the Bohemian nation.

The people of Prague then sent to Žižka in Tábor
for help. Žižka himself and 9,000 warriors and three
captains with him, started in all haste for Prague.
On the way he defeated on the River Sázava the combined armies of the King and the nobles, which tried
to bar his way, and on May 20th entered the capital.
Here he directed the defence against the overwhelming

forces of the Crusaders. The towns of Žatec, Louny and Slaný also sent help to Prague. But all this was nothing compared with the " cloud " of Sigmund's armies, which had enveloped Prague on all sides. Their camp not only extended over the Hradčany, Letná and Bubeneč, not unlike three towns of tents, but threatened Prague also from the south, where Sigmund's son-in-law was in command. There were about 150,000 troops assembled, under 40 different princes. Žižka could keep up communication with the country to the eastward alone, thanks to the timely occupation, with his Táborites, of the heights of Vítkov. The siege lasted two weeks, the crusaders committing unspeakable cruelties in the neighbourhood, among other things capturing defenceless persons and burning them alive, in order to terrify the people of Prague and force them to surrender. But the general attack did not take place till July 14th.

Then the battle of the hill of Vítkov commenced. Žižka fortified himself on Vítkov with a hastily erected block-house and personally directed the defence against the cavalry attack launched from the castle by King Sigmund. With penetrating blasts of their trumpets the cavalry dashed against Žižka, who, when the defenders of the block-house began to give way, threw himself in the first line. There was a moment when only twenty-six men still held their ground and with them a woman and a girl from Tábor, both of whom tried to beat off the Crusaders with stones. The Meissen troopers (Saxons) pulled Žižka by the legs from the wall. His danger instantly renewed the courage of the Táborites—they began to fight with such fury that the riders were soon scattered, throwing the troops behind them into hopeless confusion.

The Prague troops saw from the town walls and watch-towers the fight on Mount Vítkov, and fears ran high. The aged, the women and children knelt in prayer; the men, led by a priest carrying the Host and accompanied by the ringing of alarm bells, streamed out of the gates across the Hospital field to their brothers' assistance. When, however, Žižka's counter-attack succeeded, the German army fled towards the river to avoid being intercepted by the Prague garrison. While the Táborites pursued them from behind, the people of Prague assailed them on the flank and in a little while all was over—the defeat was overwhelming.

" Before Antichrist no true Christian shall retreat ! " exclaimed a Hussite woman defending herself against the Crusaders and dying under their blows on Mount Vítkov. Filled with grief and anger, Sigmund was obliged to withdraw from Prague, while the German princes raged both at the Bohemians and the King, for Sigmund would not permit them to bombard and reduce Prague to ruins, being still in hopes that Prague would some day become his residence. Before leaving he tried to conclude an armistice with the people of Prague, so that he could disband the German army and send it out of the country. It was a trick intended to drive a wedge between the Táborites and Prague. But the people of Prague gave him the answer, that they would do nothing without the consent of their allies.

If the battles in which Žižka had been previously victorious could be considered as of local or inferior character, his victory at Prague and the frustrated crusade carried his fame far beyond the frontiers. From that day Žižka was naturally considered the

sole military leader of the Bohemian nation, and
Mount Vítkov has ever since been known as Žižkov.
The people of Prague wished the Táborite troops to
remain with them, as they feared the King would
repeat his attacks. In the meanwhile the burghers
of Prague and the prominent men amongst the Táborites came to a confidential agreement not to regard
Sigmund as their King any longer and to call in the
Polish King Vladislaus to replace him. To this
secret agreement Žižka, in the name of the Táborites,
affixed his seal. In August the Bohemian noble
Hynek of Kolštejn was sent to Poland to King
Vladislaus.

During the temporary absence of King Sigmund
the Táborite brotherhood returned home, having some
accounts to settle with the " King of South Bohemia,"
Oldřich of Rosenberk, who laid siege to Tábor at the
moment when Sigmund was beleaguering Prague.
Although he had suffered defeat when Žižka sent from
Prague his captain Nicholas of Husi with a part of his
army, he was still very dangerous to Tábor, especially
as Sigmund had not left the country yet, but was busy-
ing himself at Kutná Hora and Čáslav with new war
preparations. So as to prevent Rosenberk from
simultaneously threatening Tábor, the Táborites began
to attack his strong places and estates in Southern
Bohemia and also greatly extended their power in the
southern and south-western districts of the kingdom.
From this time also dates the great victory won by
Žižka over the royal army at Bor near Horažd'ovice (in
October 1420), the capture of the town of Prachatice,
etc. Another Tábor captain took the two huge
Rosenberk fortresses of Příbenice and Třebeničky,
which dominated the country close to Tábor, and there

was no other course left to the Lord of Rosenberk than to allow the use of the chalice in his domains.

King Sigmund soon undertook a second expedition against Prague which was, besides, all the time in jeopardy on account of the presence of two royal garrisons, one at the Hradčany, the other at Vyšehrad. He also brought strong reinforcements of Moravian and Hungarian nobility. But again was he defeated, this time at Vyšehrad, the most distinguished leaders of the Moravian nobility being among the slain. This was on November 1st.

The first Crusade against the Bohemians failed miserably. The second, in August 1421, for which the German princes collected a much stronger army than that of the preceding year, ended in still greater ignominy. The Crusaders came as far as Žatec, behaving everywhere " with more cruelty than the heathens themselves could," but when it became known that Žižka himself was on the march against them from Prague, the German army dispersed. The report was, however, false, for Žižka who, in July, while besieging the Castle of Rábí in Southern Bohemia, had been shot in the eye so that he barely escaped with his life, had remained in Prague to have his wound attended to. The next year (1422) the third expedition of the Crusaders came to a still more inglorious end. King Sigmund made no halt throughout the whole of 1421 in his war preparations. His Hungarian and, it was said, even Tartar troops, entered and marched through Moravia, ending by the taking of the towns of Polička and Jihlava. Panic and fear spread all over Bohemia. Then the people of Prague and Žižka with his Táborites again united and defeated the King at Kutná Hora so decisively, that his army fled, without order or discipline, streaming back towards Moravia. But the Bohemians overtook the Crusaders at Německý Brod, took the town on January 10th 1422 and wreaked such a bloody vengeance on the defeated (against Žižka's will) as had never been heard of before. The town was then burned and for seven years lay desolate. The dead were said to number 12,000, their bodies being gnawed by dogs and wolves, till the peasants from the neighbourhood, moved by pity, buried them. On the following day, Sunday, January 11th 1422, Žižka was knighted before the town walls ; the only distinction, so far as we know, that was ever conferred in the Táborite army.

It would be but one-sided were we to remember Žižka merely as a warrior. The year 1421, although filled with his victorious war expeditions, especially to the north and east of Bohemia, was also filled with anxieties as to the next King. From these cares was evolved the plan to convoke a great assembly of all Utraquists at Čáslav for June 1421. The assembly was to end the devastation of the country as well as its religious disorders and to restore the country administration and general welfare. Therefore all those came who sided with Žižka and the people of Prague against the King ; the Moravian nobles and country squires, too, came ; only the Lusatians and Silesians failed to appear.

An assembly of this kind had never before been seen in the country, for not only the old Estates were there, the Catholics, *nolens volens*, among them, but also the representatives of the towns and even the delegates of the Táborites or, more properly, of armed peasants.

By its protocol of June 7th the assembly declared :

1. That the countries of Bohemia and Moravia

were Hussite and as such would defend the four articles of Prague as their common profession of faith.

2. That they would not have Sigmund for king, he being a defamer of the Hussite religious truths and an enemy to the nation, " except God should will it otherwise or another agreement should be reached between the people of Prague, the nobles, and the Táborites and others who will adhere to the four articles of Prague." Whoever should refuse to accept this (as well as the first) part of the agreement, was to be compelled to do so by force and be considered an enemy in the meanwhile.

3. The assembly renounced all obedience to the Pope of Rome and invested the theologians of Prague University with authority in all matters pertaining to the Church. It also ordered the clergy to call a synod which should establish church regulations on the basis of the articles of Prague ; to this organization the clergy should submit unanimously and also promise absolute obedience to the archbishop. Accordingly Archbishop Konrad, while still in Čáslav, summoned the synod to Prague for July 4th 1421.

4. The Estates, having deposed Sigmund, resolved to negotiate with the Polish King Vladislav and with the Great Prince of Lithuania, Vitold, that either one or the other should accept the crown of the Kingdom of Bohemia. During the interregnum, i.e. as long as a new King be not installed, there were elected twenty administrators or governors of the country, who were charged with administration and the settlement of all disputes between the municipalities, and who were also to order everything that was necessary for the defence of the kingdom. These governors were elected from the nobility, five ; country-squires, seven ;

people of Prague and the other towns, eight.   Among
the elected administrators were also two delegates of
the Tábor Brotherhood—Žižka and Buchovec.   The
members of the assembly concluded their work in
Čáslav Church by singing the *Te Deum Laudamus*.

This assembly is of great significance for the evolution of Hussitism.   Huss died for a religious idea.
But six years after his death Hussitism ceases to be
mere religious idea and becomes a synthesis of opinions,
from which then grew the whole national programme.
Likewise, attempts at a new social order were soon
made in Tábor.   The Čáslav assembly is an indication
of how deeply Hussitism had penetrated into the
temporal government of the day and how its spirit
began to shape both the national and political programme.   " It included," according to Palacký, " all
the principal affairs of public national life."

First place was taken, of course, by the law of God
and religious liberty, as defined by Huss.   The latter
again presupposed a regular organization for the
Hussite Church.   But all the other resolutions are of
a temporal kind : not to have Sigmund for a king,
because of his enmity to the Czech tongue, or in effect
the Czech nation—this indicates the aroused national
sensibility ; to give the Bohemian kingdom a ruler of
Slavonic nationality from Poland or Lithuania—a political movement.   But the most memorable is the election
of the country administrators.   There is no instance
in Europe that any of the peoples at that time had
thought it possible that they could govern themselves
by persons elected from their own midst.   The Čáslav
election is the harbinger of that representative system,
which became an idea of later ages.   In the Čáslav
election a breach was also made in the ancient custom,

which allowed only the nobility and representatives of the King's towns to be members of the diet. Already the selection of the administrators is unusual : the towns have the most representatives, the nobility the least. And, besides, two of the Tábor Brotherhood were also chosen from the ranks of those peasants who took up arms for the sake of religion and who formed the kernel of the " warriors of God." It was a progress in both idea and practice, something amazingly new in the Middle Ages.

The Čáslav assembly also illustrates how human reason, when freed from religious pressure, began to free itself in all directions : politically, economically and later also scientifically. The chain, once broken, no longer fettered. Huss raised the nameless and blind human being to a personality when he assigned to him the right to think and to make use of his intellect. It could have been expected that the increased personal dignity would gradually become a force finally convincing a man of his right to self-determination. And, behold, six years after Huss' death the accomplished fact is here. If one can see at Tábor and elsewhere how the Hussites began to think freely, to read, to establish schools and, likewise, to attempt a new economic order, one can see all this better still from the result of the Čáslav assembly. The elements of democracy were moving forward.

In June 1421 the Bohemian nation lived without Pope or King, and the sun shone down upon it just as upon all other nations. The whole world of that day trembled on hearing of such an unheard of thing. That the nation had for long paid no regard to the Pope was already well known, but that the native church should submit to the theological magisters of

Prague University as to their supreme authority—this
was something entirely new.   And yet, although
Sigmund was dethroned by the nation and the country
administration put in the hands of elected trustworthy
personages, chosen from all parties regardless of their
religion or social class, hell did not open to swallow
such miscreants !

The Čáslav Diet was the work of John Žižka and
the people of Prague, that is to say, the impulse came
from the democratic classes.   Žižka was as great a
statesman as he was warrior.   None of his contemporaries paid as much attention to the defence of, and
order in, the country as he.

Ambition had no place in Žižka's mind.   His com-
rade Nicholas of Husi was suspected of attempts
to obtain the Bohemian throne by deposing King
Václav IV and even more so after the death of the latter,
but no breath of suspicion ever touched Žižka.   It was
he, originally, who, with the people of Prague, was
most anxious the Bohemian crown should be worn by
the King of Poland, and he did not withdraw this
demand even when elected one of the country administrators.   And it was from the Čáslav assembly that a
new, and this time a public, embassy was sent to
Poland.

King Sigmund's winter expedition to Bohemia was
approaching.   At this time Žižka's supremacy was
unquestioned.   When, on December 1st 1421, he
arrived at Prague, he was welcomed with as much
pomp as formerly the King himself had been.   The
whole military preparations against Sigmund were
concentrated in his hands.   Žižka called himself the
" Administrator of the Communities of Bohemia
inclined towards and observing the law of God."   Sig-

mund's power he had destroyed at Německý Brod.
He was the most worthy of all to be made a king.
Blind he was only physically—his intellectual sight was
clear. But knowing the disposition of his countrymen, he wanted a king of noble family. His views
soon proved to be correct.

The Polish king feared to accept the Bohemian
crown on account of the Pope, but was agreeable to
its bestowal upon his cousin Vitold, who reigned in
Lithuania. Vitold first sent his nephew Sigmund
Korybut to Bohemia, as his representative. This
youth, who had no idea of either Žižka's character or
significance, insulted him grossly in a letter he wrote
him from Moravia, exhorting Žižka not to devastate
and pillage the country as he was doing. But when,
a little later, they met personally, Žižka did not recall
the insult. According to the Old Chronicler, the
prince called Žižka " father " and Žižka called the
prince " son."

Unfortunately, these relations were not of long
duration. There were two circumstances which inter-
fered with Žižka's plans, disturbing at the same time
the country's unity, which was then especially necessary. The Pope and the German Empire had agreed,
at the Imperial diet in Nuremberg, in August 1422,
on a new crusade against Bohemia. The crusaders
were to assemble on the western borders of Bohemia
on September 9th, under the leadership of Frederick
the Elector of Brandenburg. The religious extremes
of the Táborite priests began to run to excesses, which
had an evil effect on the friendly relations between
Tábor and Prague. In the New Town of Prague it
was the preacher John Želivský, who, though otherwise as bitter an enemy of Sigmund as Žižka himself,

was trying to obtain dominion over Prague with the help of the lower classes, and with that object in view was incessantly disturbing the Old, more moderate, Town and undermining the influence of Sigmund Korybut. He was a great supporter of those Táborite priests who tried to interfere with Žižka's policies. A particularly passionate priest, by name Václav Koranda, distinguished himself by his opposition to Žižka. In 1422 a breach occurred between Žižka and Tábor. Two of the later Tábor captains, Bohuslav of Švamberk and John Bzdinka of Vícemilice, broke off relations with Žižka, and on September 30th 1422 secretly entered Prague against the Old Town people. They had to withdraw without accomplishing anything, because not even the lower classes—especially of the Old Town—would join them. The extremists began to drive Prague into alliances with the most conservative elements, until the people secretly obtained the help of even the Catholic party. When finally Prince Vitold changed his mind as to the acceptance of the Bohemian crown, recalled, in December 1422, Korybut from Bohemia, and went over to Sigmund's party, Žižka's plans with regard to order in the country and its administration collapsed entirely, and he attached himself to the Oreb Brotherhood, who were in full sympathy with him.

During the anarchy that now ensued a terrible internal struggle broke out between Žižka and the people of Prague, for reasons not quite clear to us now. All we see is that on one side stood the people of Prague with the nobility loyal to Sigmund, on the other Žižka with the Horebites and Tábor, who reiterated " their willingness to obey him as ever." The object of this civil war was to destroy Sigmund's party

of nobles, which was then strongest in the east of
Bohemia, so that the people of Prague and other
towns could not look for support to it. Žižka defeated
first Čeněk of Vartenberk with his noble comrades,
in the battle of St. Gotthard near Hořice, and Švamberk the people of Prague between Vožice and Načera-
dec, after which a battle took place near Hradec Králové, which has become notorious in the history of the
Hussite wars because there " *ark went against ark*," i.e.
the Host was carried on both sides by the priests at
the head of the troops. Žižka defeated both the
people of Prague and of the towns associated with
them, and killed the priest who carried the Host on the
Prague side with his own mace.

The third crusade, agreed upon in Nuremberg,
was intended for the spring of 1423. But the whole
expedition proved sterile. Both the Polish king
Vladislaus and the Lithuanian prince Vitold were to
take part in it, but declined at the last moment. The
German princes collected only an inconsiderable number
of troops, which on reaching the Bohemian frontiers
returned owing to quarrels that broke out among the
princes. The King of Denmark, when informed of
this, withdrew from Germany with his army.

After the defeats suffered by the people of Prague
efforts at reconciliation, which are called the " disputes
on the vestments," were undertaken. The religious
contrasts between Tábor and Prague were generally
expressed by the question whether the Mass should
be read in vestments (Prague) or without vestments
(Tábor). The disputation of the theologians of both
parties, which were decided by laymen (in the presence
of the armed forces of both sides), were held on
June 24th in a field near the Castle of Konopiště. After

the heated arguments, which nearly led to a battle, had subsided, an agreement was reached to leave both sides freedom in this matter. The priests of Prague then read the Mass without vestments, the Táborites in vestments, and both sides parted in friendly spirit. And for the time being Tábor and Prague fought side by side against King Sigmund and his men. Their united army marched to Moravia, and Žižka went as far as Hungary in order to menace King Sigmund. That was in the autumn of 1423. The Hungarians did not obstruct his passage to Gran, hoping to destroy him on his return. Žižka's defence of seven days' duration on his return march in his wagon wall, against the immense Hungarian army which surrounded or outflanked him, is considered the greatest accomplishment of Žižka's strategic genius. The Hungarians themselves were filled with wonder at it and are said to have exclaimed that " he is not a man, but a devil," and the Bohemian chronicler noted : " And so the Lord God aided him in withdrawing from Hungary. But when Žižka began to fight (here), it was the hardest for him."

During Žižka's expeditions into the Bohemian provinces and also during his punitive expedition to Hungary, the harmony between the people of Prague and both the Utraquist and Catholic nobility had made considerable progress. The connection between Tábor and Prague had previously been maintained by the fanatical preacher John Želivský, who was now dead, the people of Prague having treacherously executed him on March 9th 1422. After his death Prague became more and more estranged from Žižka. On June 11th Žižka found it necessary to threaten the people of Prague. Thus we read in

one of his letters : " And if . . . ye should encourage
any storms or any lies and quarrels, that occur between
the towns, any longer, then we will, with the help of
God and our prince's (Korybut's) grace, and together
with the councillors and other lords, knights, squires
and all faithful towns, do our part and take revenge on
every one, without exception. . . ."

It is evident that it was nothing but prudence which
caused Žižka, as early as 1423, to organize a standing
army ready to strike at any moment. For himself
he organized a Little Tábor in the Hradec country,
leaving Great Tábor in command of his friend John
Hvězda. In time of war, however, both Brotherhoods were under the supremacy of Žižka. In October 1423 there was imminent danger that between the
people of Prague and the Catholic nobles on one side
and the Brotherhoods on the other side, nothing but
the sword could decide. The St. Galli diet of the
people of Prague and the nobles in Prague ended in
an agreement that it was necessary to re-establish the
administration of the country, as drawn up in Čáslav
in 1423, and twelve administrators were thereupon
elected, to the exclusion of the armies of the Brotherhoods. Not content with this, the diet engaged itself
to make war on *the destroyers of the country*, meaning
the Táborites and Horebites. This was a declaration
of war. Žižka on his return from Hungary had time
to defeat the Catholic nobles at Česká Skalice, but in
1424 he found himself hard pressed when the people
of Prague and the nobles hemmed him in at Kostelec
on the Labe. He was practically defeated and was
only saved by the timely arrival of Hynek Boček of
Kunštát, who was then captured himself.

Before the battle of Česká Skalice Žižka was in

danger of being murdered. On November 24th
1423 he received, from the mayor and councillors of
Hradec Králové, a letter written by the hand of their
parochial priest, Ambrose, to the effect that they had
" taken prisoner a man of some importance, hailing
from the neighbourhood of Opočno," who betrayed to
them that there was somebody in Žižka's camp who
was conspiring to murder him, for which deed he was
hired for forty sacks of groats.   The messenger who
delivered the letter, one " Paul with the black head,"
happened to know the hired assassin, and was to point
him out to Žižka and also to tell him by whom he was
hired.   Unfortunately we know nothing more about
this disclosure nor its outcome.

During this fighting with the people of Prague in
the first week of June, Žižka, seeing himself greatly
outnumbered, avoided contact with the enemy till he
found a favourable position, at Malešov near Kutná
Hora, where he split the enemy's forces in two and
then crushed them.   Having occupied a hill, he had
wagons filled with stones rolled down into the midst
of the enemy surrounding him.   The people of
Prague alone lost 1,200 men, the nobles and knights
having also suffered greatly in both killed and
wounded.   This happened on June 7th 1424.

That summer witnessed discord among those who
had participated in the St. Galli diet in Prague the
year before.   The people of Prague and the Utraquist
nobles once more enticed Korybut to Bohemia, offering him the crown.   The Utraquist (Calixtines) party
withdrew its allegiance to the twelve administrators
whom it had helped to elect in the diet, and the Catholic party again refused to take orders from Korybut.
Nevertheless, the resolution in regard to the " de-

stroyers of the country" was not revoked. Žižka
having in the meantime strengthened the Táborite
positions all over the country by a number of expeditions, suddenly appeared, in September 1424, before
Prague, encamping at the village of Libeň near by.
The people of Prague were horror stricken. But
there were also many in the Brotherhoods who thought
with consternation of the consequences should " ark
go against ark " once more. In the end an embassy
was sent from Prague to conciliate Žižka. The
reconciliation succeeded, it is said, after the patriotic
speech of a young priest named John Rokycana
(September 14th), who held at Prague the important
place formerly held by John Želivský. As a sign of
the reconciliation a mound of stones was piled up at
Libeň. Korybut remained the administrator of
the Prague party, and Žižka of the Brotherhoods,
pending future agreements. But Žižka did not trust
the people of Prague even after the conclusion of the
peace pact. He said : " There will be as much
peace as after the reconciliation at Konopiště," refer-
ring, undoubtedly, to the quarrels about the vestments.

The allied forces of Žižka and Korybut took the
field in October, an army of 20,000 setting out for
Moravia.

When laying siege to the town and Castle of Přibyslav, Žižka died (on October 11th), at the very moment
when it seemed that the results for which he had fought
so victoriously during the last four years would be
attained. Korybut sent, while on this expedition, a
challenge to King Sigmund, in which he called himself
King of Bohemia by request and election, and declared
that he would defend the four articles of Prague and
that he would uphold the Bohemian nation in all

things. Thus the prospects of the Bohemians having a king of their own and of eternally repudiating the " red-haired knave," whom Žižka would never have allowed to occupy the Bohemian throne, were good indeed at the time when Žižka died suddenly of plague.

The Old Chronicler wrote of him this plain and touching eulogy : " Here (at Přibyslav) Brother John Žižka fell mortally ill with the plague and left as a last behest to his dear brothers and Bohemians, the Lord Viktorin, and the knights John Bzdinka and Kuneš that they, fearing our dear Lord, should always and faithfully defend the truth of God for the eternal reward. And then Brother Žižka, recommending his soul to God, departed this life the Wednesday before St. Galli. And then his people assumed the name of Sirotci (orphans), as if a father of theirs had died. . . . And then the priest Ambrož accompanied Brother Žižka, being dead, to Hradec Králové and there they laid him to rest by the high altar in the Church of St. Anna."

This threefold watchword resounds throughout the whole of Žižka's activity : *the law of God* (that is, Hussitism and the defence of the four articles of Prague) ; *the defence of the country* (the unity of all Calixtines against Rome and Sigmund) ; and the *common welfare* (the maintenance of order in the kingdom).

The maintenance of the common welfare is to be credited to John Žižka's statesmanship. This part of his labours was unnoticed by his contemporaries, but not by his descendants of the nineteenth century when they contemplated his deeds. His statesmanship manifested itself by his intervention in the internal disputes of the country. He frequently left the battlefield to go either to Tábor or Prague, where his personal intercession was needed by both sides. But we recognize his statesmanship even better in the manner in which, after the battle on Mount Vítkov, he came to an understanding with the people of Prague to the effect that they would call to the throne the Polish King Vladislaus. The Čáslav diet of 1421 was also Žižka's work. This explains why the whole country looked up to Žižka and why his policy became generally accepted. Now we understand why he was greeted in Prague, on December 1st 1421, with such pomp as was the King himself on other occasions, at a time when he was no more than the " administrator of the communities in Bohemia." Korybut, as the representative of the King, obtained, in 1422, the recognition of the country because Žižka stood behind him despite the grumbling of some Táborites. And when the year 1423 brought the Kingdom of Bohemia into a new situation, Žižka warned the people of Prague not to accept the vacillating Prince Vitold of Lithuania as their King, declaring that he, Žižka, would protect them and take care that, being free, they should have no need of any King at all. We shall never learn what it was that Žižka then had in mind.

But Žižka, the invincible general, pushed Žižka the statesman into the background. As a leader and warrior he abided in the memory of his nation to the exclusion of anything else. Not long after his death a small book was issued, with the title *The Handsome Chronicle of John Žižka, the Servant of King Václav*, a delightful pamphlet for its simplicity and primitiveness. It is full of admiration for Žižka's victories and of affection for his personality.

" At that time there arose a Bohemian of the knightly
order and very brave, a one-eyed man called Žižka, by
the grace of God, and he rose and marched in war-
order against those who would not receive the body
of Christ in both kinds. For them he esteemed as
enemies and scorned them as heretics. . . ."

" And Žižka marched in war-order through the
country, taking castles and towns. And many fights
he had with the enemy, but never did he lose the
field. . . ."

" But then at Přibyslav a plague fell upon Žižka,
and he died and they buried him in Hradec Králové,
and there he lies. Then they renamed his troops
Sirotci (orphans), and thus they were called ever afterwards. And the people of Hradec had painted on
their banner the likeness of Žižka, sitting on a white
horse in knightly armour with a mace in his hand, as
he used to ride forth when alive. And whenever the
people of Hradec fought beneath that banner, they
never lost their fight."

Of his statesmanship the little book says nothing.
For to his people Žižka was primarily a Gideon, who,
with a small number of peasants, slew the hosts of the
Midians. The sword of the Lord and of Gideon was
victorious ! And one more virtue of Žižka's was
always extolled—his entire absence of avarice, indeed
his virtual poverty. Born the son of a country squire,
he died a poor knight. His victories offered him
many opportunities of enriching himself, and yet he
only kept a poor fort near Litoměřice, where he could
scarcely ever even rest. The fort was called Kalich
(chalice), from which he and his brother both signed
" of Kalich," but as for a revenue from that possession
of his, such a thing was non-existent. After his

death, his aunt was given a pension by the municipality of Prague.

Two contemporary writers familiar with the events of his life characterized Žižka in a manner that would furnish suitable epitaphs for his grave. Vavřinec of Březová, though not friendly to him, wrote : " A rare zealot for the law of Christ." And the Old Chronicler : " . . . with whom God was all the time, for being his faithful servant." Modern investigators of Žižka's life—Tomek and Toman—are in full agreement with the old witnesses. Dr. Hugo Toman, who also wrote an extensive work on the Hussite warfare, says in regard to Žižka's character : " He that incurred Žižka's enmity will not be left unscathed by the moral judgment of history. . . ."

It is well known that the national movement also played a rôle in Huss' trial at Constance. He was described by the Germans as a Germanophobe. The Old Chronicler, too, added at the time of the German exodus from Prague University in 1409 that : " Then when Magister John Huss came to Constance, they blamed him for that, and it also was largely the reason of his death." In a like manner Žižka is occasionally accused of massacring the Germans. Even one of the German historians, Dr. Konstantin Höfler—who under the Austrian regime was, on account of his views, appointed Rector of Prague University—repudiated not only Huss and the whole Hussite religious movement, but even declared that the Bohemians used religion only as a pretext for massacring the hated Germans and for driving them from the country.

In order thoroughly to understand Huss, Žižka and the Hussites, it is first necessary to say a word about the Germans both in Bohemia and Moravia.

It was an evil heritage that the Přemyslides left to
the nation. They greatly Germanized their own
family by frequent marriages with German princesses.
One of them even was a German poet. Until the
thirteenth century the population of the Bohemian
territories was purely Czech, except for the western
corner of the Loket county with its handful of German
villages, bordering on the German district of Eger
(Cheb). The thirteenth century witnessed a new
migration of the Germans towards the east, especially
from the over-populated western portion of Germany.
The Germans pressed into Bohemia, Poland and even
Hungary, and it suited the Přemyslides to settle
them in the country, partly in the sparsely inhabited
section, partly in the mining districts, for the colonists
brought the royal house great profit. The revenues obtained from the new German settlements, by Přemysl II
and Václav II particularly, were extremely high.
The Germans occupied, first of all, the royal border
forest—where they are still settled—and founded also
large settlements in the interior, to which the kings
granted the privileges of the German municipal law.
The best known German town was the mining town of
Kutná Hora. In course of time the isolated settlements of Germans grew into districts of considerable
extent, where the Czech element was in the minority
both as to numbers and property. And, let us add, that
the last Přemyslides reigned also in the German Alpine
countries and in Saxony. Following the example of
their sovereigns, the Czech nobles and the large monasteries enriched themselves through the colonists,
whom they settled on their lands besides assisting
them in founding small towns.

The first complaints against the German settlers

were heard in the beginning of the fourteenth century, under the Luxemburg dynasty, and that from among the nobility (*vide* Dalemil's chronicle) who began to feel the expansive force of the German burghers, especially in Prague and Kutná Hora. The domineering German character irritated the Czechs no less. Already into an older translation of the St. Anselm legend the Bohemian translator inserted the following resentful verse :

> " Jídáš byl taký lakomec
> někteří tomu chtěli, že byl Němec
> (Judas was such a miser
> that some averred he was a German)."

Dalemil in his chronicle rebuked the Přemyslides on every opportunity for their German predilections, and warned his countrymen of the troublesome German strangers. The new Luxemburg dynasty, being more or less French, did not show any preference for the Germans, but accepted the existing conditions. In Prague the councilmen were, as a rule, mostly German, and many State offices, high and low, were held by them. But the German influence weighed most heavily on Prague University, which Charles IV had organized in such a way that the so-called " Bohemian nation " had one vote, the foreign " nations " three, and in all these three foreign nations the Germans were in the majority. The opposition to the Germans began to grow as early as the time of Charles IV, thus prior to Hussitism. Our chronicler, Martin Lupáč, notes : " Anno Domini 1377. The Germans who, under Charles IV, have grown much in Prague, caused the burghers, neighbours and inhabitants of Prague many and frequent disputes and spiteful displeasures, which led to serious troubles between the native Bohemians and the immigrant Germans, so that they had often to be brought before the Imperial Majesty ! "

Can, then, anybody wonder that a born Czech from South Bohemia and a preacher among the people should, like the majority of his countrymen, feel the national humiliation of the hegemony (certainly not an amiable one) of the German minority of that period over the native Bohemian majority ? We cannot wonder that Huss preached not only a divine, but also a national, justice. Something in this respect we have already heard. When, in 1409, he defended the decree of Kutná Hora, he also gave this explanation of his views: "At the commencement of learning (University learning) the Bohemians were but weak in the sciences, and thus, for lack of knowledge, were like servants to the Germans till the time set by the Father —i.e. Emperor Charles—who used to say : ' Not until you mature in the sciences, will you be the masters and heirs too, just wait a little ! ' But now that, with the help of God, the time has arrived when the Czech teachers are more numerous than the German and when they rise in all the sciences and abilities above the foreigners, it follows that they are servants no more, but sons, and, because sons, therefore also heirs through God. Let, then, all those stewards and protectors withdraw who seek to profit from the heirs to the Kingdom, and may the heirs, to whom the heritage belongs, live for all eternity !

" And the German nation surely would not suffer the Bohemian nation to hold the higher place in Vienna or Heidelberg or to be the leader there, and always at the head. And as the German nation would desire to hold a higher place than the Bohemian in Vienna or Heidelberg, thus it should not, on the one hand, desire the higher place in Bohemia, while on the other hand it should desire the Bohemian nation to be, in the country of Bohemia, higher than the other nations, and that it be the head and not the tail, and always above and not below. This was confirmed even by our Redeemer, when He said : Do unto others as ye would they should do unto you. If, then, the Germans wish the Bohemians, when in Germany, to act so as not to interfere with their councils, votes and welfare and not to put themselves above or desire to be the head, so they (the Germans) should, when in Bohemia, do unto the Bohemians.

"And the Germans who are in Bohemia should go before the king and swear fealty to him and the country. But that will happen only when the snake shall warm itself on ice."

Thus spoke Huss while explaining the Ten Commandments. Yet at the same time he said : " I declare on my conscience, that if I knew a foreigner, no matter from whence, and his virtues, and that he loved God and the virtues better than my own brother, he would be dearer to me than my own brother. And therefore good English priests are dearer to me than faint-hearted Bohemian priests and a good German dearer than a mean brother."

That he was a patriot, without being a Chauvinist, can be also said of Žižka. When he gave to his Brotherhood (in 1423) his spiritual as well as his temporal regulations, he concluded with the words that he undertook everything—" for our dear Lord God, for his sacred martyrdom, for the liberation of the truth of the law of God, the saints and their praise, for aiding the faithful to the Holy Church, and especially for the Czech and Slovak language."

Bartošek of Drahonice, a Bohemian mercenary, who, being a Catholic, fought the Hussites with both pen and sword, did not hesitate to write of the Habsburg Albrecht II : " He was not a bad man, although a German." Evidently the Germans were disliked by the Bohemian Catholics too.

How much the more, then, must they have been disliked by the Hussites ! For, while Huss and the greater part of the nation were burning with ardour for Church reforms, the Germans at the University and on the Prague town council played as long as possible the unenviable rôle of reactionaries. This was why Huss and his friends, with the assistance of King Václav IV, broke their power at the University. The decree of Kutná Hora gave the Bohemian nation three votes, leaving one to the Germans, and this decision, being indisputably just, was lauded by the whole nation. Hurt in their pride, the Germans then departed from Prague and founded a university at Leipzig, the first high school of Germany, and one which, for a long time, was devoid of any significance.

When, after Huss' death, the appeal to arms was made in Prague, the German burghers fled from the town *en masse*, leaving their houses to fate. They felt insecure before the wrath of the people, who remembered how the German councillors had decapitated three youths for having insulted the indulgences, although they gave Huss their word of honour that they would not hurt them. They also fled from other towns. At that time Hussitism was already called the Bohemian faith ; Catholicism, the German faith.

Nothing, however, could be done for the relief of

the panic-stricken Germans. The German princes were the first who, inspired by the Pope, hung a cross on their breast as a symbol against the heretics. Can then anybody wonder at the contents of the manifesto of the Prague people in 1420, which called the nation to arms against the Germans in these words—" whom, although for no reason whatever, our tongue always makes angry and who, as they have done with our tongue on the Rhine, in Saxony and Prussia, from where they have banned it, so they intend to do to us and occupy the places of the exiles."

The Hussite wars broke the German hegemony in Prague and other towns. This meant the Czechizing of the interior of Bohemia, even the pushing of the Germans as far as the frontiers. The Hussites did not aim at troubling the Germans when they behaved peaceably. But that both the Bohemian and Slavonic consciousness was awaked is self-evident.

It is the national question, then, with which the accusations of cruelty made against the Calixtines, and especially the Táborites, are connected. Of course blood was shed. Wars are not made with gloved hands even now, and even less so in the fifteenth century, when the encounter was a personal, man-to-man contest. Unbiased historians, however, have ascertained that the cruelty on the part of the native Catholics and, even more so, on the part of the foreign crusaders was far worse, more inhuman, than on the side of the Hussites. This is intelligible enough, when we bear in mind that the Pope promised remission of sins to every one who would kill a Bohemian. So they killed Bohemians wherever they found them—not only soldiers, but peasants in the fields, defenceless women and babies. A Hussite had then to defend himself and to kill, in his turn, since he was defending his fatherland and the truth that was sown in it.

It was Huss and Žižka who founded the historic glory of Hussitism. Huss has lived in the memory of the nation as the "reverend preacher." He has sown among the nation the seed of a better religious knowledge. Žižka, the unconquered leader, transformed the country into an armed camp and by defeating its opponents saved the Bohemian nation from extinction.

IV

Peter Chelčický, the Thirteenth Apostle

ALTHOUGH Žižka drove out three crusading expeditions from Bohemia, the consummation of his victories was left to his successors, to the priest Prokop the Bald (otherwise called Prokop the Great) in particular.

The last Crusades against the Bohemians ended with increasing ignominy to the Crusaders. In 1427 Pope Martin summoned the German princes for a new Crusade, and as its leader appointed the English Bishop of Winchester, Henry Beaufort, giving him simultaneously the Cardinal's hat. This Cardinal was selected partly for his being related to the royal family. The crusading army first laid siege to the town of Stříbro, but when the Bohemian troops came within about three miles of the besieged town, the Crusaders were seized with panic and fled (August 27th). The Cardinal succeeded in stopping at least a part of the army near Tachov, where he unfurled the papal standard, yet as the Bohemians were heard approaching, there was a repetition of the flight at Stříbro and the Cardinal himself narrowly escaped being captured.

King Sigmund thereupon started peace negotiations with the Bohemians, trying to induce the Hussites to carry the dispute about their doctrines before the

Church Council, which was shortly to meet in Basle.

Not so Pope Martin.   This most inveterate enemy
of the heretics aroused Europe to undertake for the
year 1431 the largest expedition yet raised against the
Bohemians.   The German princes as well as the free
cities were burning with desire for revenge, the more
so because Prokop the Great, with an army of 10,000
men, had marched, in 1429 and 1430, through Central
Germany, spreading the terror of his unconquerable
warriors everywhere.   Even Hamburg and Lüneburg
began to fortify themselves, fearing the Hussites might
appear at their gates.   According to our Chronicler,
it was a " beautiful ride to Germany, the like of which
the Bohemians had never made before."   The Pope
secured the support of Sigmund when he induced the
German Imperial Diet to make an expedition to
Bohemia.   The Pope consented, apparently unwil-
lingly, to the summoning of the Council to Basle, and
then only in order to help King Sigmund.   But the
Bohemians had to be humbled before the Council
could meet, in spite of the fact that Sigmund had
already won their consent to his going to Basle.   Prokop the Great, the real military dictator of the country,
assembled for its defence 50,000 infantry and 500
horsemen, while the Crusaders numbered 90,000 infantry and 40,000 cavalry.   Pope Martin did not live
long enough to see a victory gained, and his successor,
Eugenius IV, was taught an unexpected lesson by the
Bohemians. Cardinal Julian Cesarini, who led the
crusading expedition, proceeded no farther than the
frontier town of Domažlice.   On August 14th, in
company with the Duke of Saxony, he ascended a high
hill so as to see the battle.   But no sooner was the song
" Ye who are warriors of God " heard from afar, when

the German cavalry began to disperse, the camp of the infantry fell into disorder and the wagoners flung away their loads. If the Bishop of Würzburg had not, during the flight, pulled the Cardinal into his own troop and disguised him as a common soldier, Julian Cesarini would not have escaped with his life. In the Šumava forest began a pursuit and slaughter of the fleeing Crusaders, a plundering of their deserted camp and a seizure of booty, among which Cesarini's cardinal's hat was an object of much merriment to the victors.

This Cardinal Cesarini now became the most ardent advocate of the idea that it was impossible to vanquish the Bohemians with the sword, as was once advised by Gerson, and that the Church must treat with them for some kind of an agreement. Thus the Council of Basle invited the Bohemians for October 15th, and the Bohemians started to negotiate. The Council of Basle was dissolved by Pope Martin in 1418, without having made the necessary Church reforms. It only helped the papacy. Pope Martin saw himself compelled to summon the Council of Basle again—in June 1431.

With this fateful autumn of 1431 begins that chapter of Bohemian history which belongs to its saddest period. The narrative of the years 1431 to 1448 caused much sorrow to the descendants of the victorious Hussites and causes regret to this day.

As the desire for peace was universal, the delegates of the Basle Council succeeded in utilizing this mood to win over certain influential persons among the Bohemians, nobles as well as townspeople. But they insisted that the responsibility for the war lay with the Táborites and Horebites, who were irreconcilable.

Although Prokop the Great was among the fifteen Bohemian envoys who, on January 4th 1433, sailed by boat to Basle, he realized, unfortunately too late, that the Council acted in an insincere and deceitful way and that all that the Bohemian nobility and the towns were doing only concealed the secret intrigue—to get rid of the Brotherhood armies. These conservative elements had formed the " League for the Restoration of Peace and Order in the Country," which the Catholics also joined, and the Brotherhoods were ordered to disperse.

The decision was entrusted to the sword at the battle at Lipany, a battle accursed and wept over for centuries. On May 30th 1434 this terrible battle at Lipany, east of Prague, took place, in which ark went against ark for the last time, and the ark of the Brotherhoods was destroyed, not by valour, but by stratagem. Bohemian outwitted Bohemian in the interests of Rome.

If the negotiations of the Church fathers with the heretic Bohemians were deceitful from the very start, they became, after the defeat of the democratic Brotherhoods, directly provocative. For the terror inspired by the victorious arms of Prokop the Great and Prokůpek (Prokop the Lesser), both of whom were killed at Lipany, had disappeared. Even the victors in that battle already began to realize that the Council was playing them false and were about to stop further negotiations. At that moment the old enemy, King Sigmund, stepped in between them. He promised the Bohemians all that they wished as soon as he should become king, and guaranteed this promise under seal. But to the Council he secretly engaged himself not to keep his promise. The meagre results of the nego-

tiations between the Bohemians and the Council were
finally issued under the name of the Compacts, which
were publicly proclaimed in Jihlava on July 6th 1436.
On the basis of these Compacts King Sigmund issued
a Letter of Majesty to the Bohemians in which he confirmed all the old rights of the people (including the
Compacts) and then made his entry into Prague. The
Compacts became part of the law of the country and its
misfortune for nearly 200 years.

The Compacts guaranteed to the Bohemians in the
main, the contents of the Four Articles of Prague, with
an addition that filled them with an exultant confi-
dence, the provision, namely, that in spite of these
exceptions *they were recognized as true and faithful sons
of the Church*. This assurance they had engraved in
Bohemian, Latin, Magyar and German, on a marble
slab, which was then placed in the Church of Corpus
Christi on the Charles Square in Prague. The negotiations regarding some of the minor Bohemian
demands, as well as about certain regulations touching
the execution of the Compacts, were left for a later date,
especially the demand that the Council of Basle should
send a letter to all countries to clear the reputation of
the Bohemians, and also that Archbishop Rokycana,
who had been elected in the meantime, should be confirmed by the Pope. King Sigmund promised the
Bohemians, with no intention of keeping his promise,
however, that he himself would be responsible for
these matters.

Of the promises made at Basle none were ever ful-
filled, the one regarding the letter clearing the Bohemian heretics in particular was disregarded. King
Sigmund entered Prague in great state on August 23rd
and at once began a savage campaign against Hus-

sitism (ordering, for example, the Táborite captain, Roháč of Dubé, to be hanged). The entire treatment of the Bohemians by the Council had been underhand from the start. This fact was betrayed as early as 1433 by the Basle auditor John Palomar, when, in a confidential circle, he came forward with this advice : " The Bohemians must be treated nicely, like horses or mules when they are being tamed, until the halter is thrown over their head. For then only, and not before, can they be tied to the crib."

Consternation was first aroused among the Bohemians when King Sigmund proved himself perfidious to the extent of even brazen shamelessness. A second cause arose when Pope Eugenius IV refused to confirm the Compacts, although it was owing to the letters he had sent to the lords and knights, to the people of Prague and other towns, in which he evinced his joy at their conciliatory behaviour, that the Compacts were successfully negotiated. But the Bohemians had a King now, the wars were over and done with.

During this period of decay, there was no occupation left for the heirs of Žižka and both the Prokops. At home there was no work for warriors. Their time did not return till during the crusades against the Hussite King.

Not all the Hussite warriors were patriots and good men, who considered the brandishing of the sword their religious and national duty. Nor were they all wise and statesmanlike people who could understand that every era requires its own methods, and what the bleeding country needed was treatment by peaceful methods. Among the warriors there were some nobles impatient for booty that could be obtained by robbery, and to these war was a profession. There were also many peasants who learned to love the soldier's life and scorned to follow the plough.

Thus arose military bands which called themselves brotherhoods, or " little brothers." A ruler as astute as King Sigmund was the first to foresee that even after Lipany the Táborite bands would remain a perpetual danger to his government. So when the Táborites were still divided on the question whether to acknowledge Sigmund as their King or not, Sigmund started negotiations with one of their chiefs. This took place before the Jihlava diet and most likely in the Táborite town of Třebič, situated on the road to Jihlava. Sigmund's amiability was, on that occasion, so great that it roused both suspicion and distrust ; he protested that he had long been favourably disposed towards the Táborites and that he had always wished to be reconciled to them, but was hindered in that by others. He even denounced the Roman hierarchy and the greed and pride of the clergy, which he pretended to have seen and experienced at the Council of Constance, at his coronation in Rome, and finally at Basle ; he also asserted that he had always been in favour of Church reforms, but could do nothing alone against the multitude of those differing with him on that point ; but that he now desired to come to an agreement with the Táborites—not through agents, whose love of peace could never be so great as his, but directly, in order to secure their co-operation once the Compacts were introduced in the whole kingdom. All these advances, however, made no other impression on the Táborites than to cause them to think that the King desired to deceive them and lead them to some place in order to perish by the sword. The fearless

Táborite captain, Roháč of Dubé, cut short Sigmund's negotiations then and there.

But though Sigmund failed at that time, his objects were accomplished by other agents, among whom was Sigmund's daughter-in-law, a few years afterwards. This widow of King Albrecht, in order to save Hungary for her son (Ladislaus Posthumus), took the remnants of Prokop the Great's field armies into her service. Among the leaders of these troops or brotherhoods two gained great renown for themselves : the distinguished Jan Jiskra of Brandýs, in the north of Hungary (Slovakia), and Jan Bítovský, in Croatia. Both ruled their territories as practically independent princes. They not only upheld the claims of Ladislaus Posthumus, but also obtained the right to use the Bohemian tongue in Hungary, and in this way considerably strengthened the Slavonic consciousness in the south of Hungary as well as in Slovakia.

A few years afterwards we find the Táborite troops in almost every part of Europe. They assisted in the quarrels over the succession in Brunswick, Westphalia, Poland and Austria, so that the Bohemian art of war spread all over Central Europe and its reputation over the whole of Europe. This even gave rise to a belief that the military camps of the Cossacks in Ukraine had their origin in the art and the instruction carried there by the Bohemians.

To the Bohemian nation, however, these mercenary soldiers were of no benefit whatever. The hatred of the heretics was only strengthened by all the devastation they committed and the fear which they inspired, especially among the German people. The effects of all this were best felt by the expedition of 1447, when it was returning from Westphalia. The

THE MARTYRDOM OF HUSS.

[*To face p.* 128

prince whom they were assisting left the expedition
in the centre of Germany without pay and in distress.
In order to get home, they practically had to cut their
way through. They suffered bitter want, and their
horses dropped through starvation. " The devil may
trust the Germans," cries our Old Chronicler angrily.

It was only with much hesitation that the magisters
of Prague assented to a mere defensive war, and during
the first fights, defensive as they were, even the synod
of the Táborite priests declared that a Christian should
always be directed by the New Testament. In particular, the Táborite priests were not allowed to touch
arms. The fierce Táborite priest, Koranda, although
he only assisted the warriors at the siege of the Rosen-
berg castle Přibenice, by throwing stones, is recalled
in the records as follows : " And on the supposition
that he might have killed somebody, he was not permitted to serve Mass, only to preach."
This small nucleus of Christian men grew in numbers during the fifteen years of the war. From it
there arose Peter Chelčický, a teacher of the peaceful
life, a " true Bohemian doctor," as he was called in
Bohemia for centuries afterwards.
Chelčický was a villager, a free peasant from the
village of Chelčice near Vodňany, about whose private
life we have but scant information. We know neither
the date of his birth nor that of his death. All we
know is that he was a self-taught man who knew very
little Latin, but that, being a religious enthusiast, he
used to go to the learned magisters in Prague for information. Huss' works he knew well, of Wyclif's
he had a second-hand knowledge. As he wrote in one
of his letters to the Bishop at Tábor : " It is possible

that in the many Latin words of Wyclif there may be
something too, although all those who read his books
say that he composed them in a heavy and concise
language. And though I could give only a small
or slight testimony in regard to Latin, yet I possess
some exposition of Magister Huss and of others,
especially that which you call, in Latin, *sacramentaliter*,
and, in Czech, sacramentally, that such a language can
be sometimes understood as meaning a figure and then
again as the matter being figured, when two sub-
stances which are joined together are spoken of. As
one of the masters, when discussing the matter, has
simply expressed it, ' that the body of Christ is not in
the sacrament physically, with all its limbs, but it is
there sacramentally, etc.' "

He might have known the works of another South
Bohemian country squire, Thomas of Štítné, a country
philosopher of the pre-Hussite period, and he had
probably heard Huss' sermons when the latter lived
in exile at Kozí Hrádek and the neighbourhood.
Certain it was, however, that in 1420 Chelčický was in
Prague and also that later he had some conversation
with the elected Hussite archbishop Rokycana. It
was to him that Peter Payne went to seek refuge when,
in 1437, he was publicly expelled from Prague.

But he lived in solitude at Chelčice, quite close to
Tábor. He became acquainted with the doctrines of
both Prague and Tábor, neither of which would satisfy
him, and also often conversed with Martin Lokvis,
the priest, as well as with Bishop Nicholas ; yet with
their views of the holy sacrament he could not agree,
as witness the following words of his : " I loved you
always above the other priests, therefore I pity you
more than the others ! "

At last he worked out his own religious system, which has made him famous in Bohemian religious history. According to this system (1) the world should be founded solely on the Gospel ; (2) if the world were arranged in conformity with Christ's plans, humanity would need no temporal organization, that is, States with political offices, courts, authorities and armies, for the State is nothing but organized violence ; (3) but after it had already happened—and that was when poison was poured into the cup of Christ, i.e. when Emperor Constantine, although a pagan, was admitted by Pope Sylvester to the faith, for which the Pope was again admitted to temporal power—since that time the imperial and papal power support, intertwine with, and mutually uphold each other, which tends to destroy pure religion. In circumstances like these the Christian should know how to behave. Thus the main idea of Chelčický was the problem which, in another form, worries even modern society, that is the relations between Church and State.

It was not until he was well advanced in years that Chelčický began to write. He was entirely lacking in literary ambition ; for as he later explained to Rokycana, " he began to write only on being urged on by many ; he feared to do so knowing well that he was too far behind others on account of his late start and of dealing only with the past ; not for the sake of peace, but rather to cause quarrels and uncertainty, as if catching a shadow that runs away from me." All his works were written between the years 1433–1443. He died somewhere in the 'fifties, in the reign of Ladislaus Posthumus. The clearest and fullest view of all that Peter taught is comprised in his bulky work *Net of the Faith*.

The following are the main tenets of Chelčický's teaching :

The Apostles founded a Church that was perfect, and should serve as a model for the Christian of all ages. The first Christians, though separating themselves from the Jews and pagans, lived among pagans and under pagan authorities ; to them the Christian was subject in matters temporal, paid taxes and obeyed their laws. Among themselves the Christians were on terms of equality and owed no duty to each other but love. Christian did not reign over Christian. When, occasionally, differences arose between the Christians which had their origin in human imperfection, the Church elders settled them by advising the repair of wrong. To a Christian who would go to the court when he felt himself injured, St. Paul taught that the death of Jesus was of no avail. Christ, like Paul, taught that we should admonish sinners with good words and, should they disregard the warning, shun them, but never force them or punish them.

The law of Christ is sufficient for Christians for all times, and it was sufficient in the fifteenth century too. Should anybody think that the Church had grown better since apostolic times, he was mistaken. The perfection of the Church lasted 300 years, up to the time of Emperor Constantine and Pope Sylvester. These two were the whales which entered the net of the faith and tore it so that now only tatters hang down from it. From that time the domination of Christian over Christian begins, from that time the Church is divided into the masters and defenders ; into priests, or those who pray, and oppressed people—the workers. The Pope was the first to begin : he forsook poverty, a life of toil and preaching, and instead arrogated to

himself the power of forgiving sins, started pilgrimages
to Rome to obtain money, invented purgatory and the
sale of indulgences, and abolished the communion in
both kinds, which was ordered by Christ Himself.
In combining temporal power with the Church both
the Emperor and Pope sinned. The ruin brought
over the Church by these two " whales " Chelčický
describes and condemns in the second half of his *Net
of the Faith*. All that disagrees with Christianity is,
according to him :

1. The aristocracy, people proud of their noble
birth and their ridiculous coats of arms. To the life
of the aristocracy he devotes chapters full of scorn and
contempt for their life of luxury.

2. The towns and their inhabitants, resembling the
aristocracy. The town organization is nothing but
robbery, violence, murder, venality, usury, adultera-
tion of goods, etc. And all this Antichrist covered
with the mantle of Christianity.

3. The worst Church institution is that of the
Mendicant Friars ; they vow poverty, but lead a life
of luxury and adorn the churches with splendour, con-
ducting also divine services with great pomp in order
to ensnare the common people.

4. The university magisters are not defenders of
Christ's faith, but perverters of the divine law. They
are joined in this by the parish priests, whose only
object is to extort money from the people.

But the rule of Christ has no need of temporal
power, for Christ's rule was fixed by God Himself,
temporal power by the people. Temporal government gains its object by compulsion, while faith cannot
be enforced. Christians have only one king and that
is Christ. If the world would acknowledge Him for

its king temporal kings would be superfluous. Sin would then disappear from the world for love of the king Christ, there would be peace on earth and law would dissolve in love.

For such people, of course, who are not under the rule of Christ, temporal rule is necessary. Because, if there were no kings and no compelling power among such people, a war of all against all would soon arise and the human race would become extinct. In a world where Christ is not king law comes to supersede law. Then, of course, law becomes to the Christians an object of gain. If the law is good and an aid to justice, to the peace of the country, and common welfare, Christians will partake in all these good things. But if the law, by being wrong, becomes oppressive, then it lets the Christians suffer and helps them to win eternal life.

Despite the fact that for bad people temporal power is necessary, and of benefit to the Christians at least in some things, a Christian must not resort to temporal power even if he desires to reform bad people. Christ cares not for good that is enforced but for the good that is voluntary.

Official position brings the Christian into the danger of doing wrong either from ignorance, favour or disfavour, and even from the love of gain. Such is the spirit of the New Testament. John the Baptist did not condemn the soldiery (Luke iii. 14), because he knew only the Old Testament. Christ, on the other hand, condemned it and taught that evil was not to be repaid with evil.

The views held by the Church of Rome as to temporal power are erroneous. True, St. Paul exhorts Christians to submit to the authorities (Romans xiii.)

and thus approves of authority. But this was done only from prudence, so that the Christians should not bring upon their heads the anger of the pagan power, not of the Christian power, as that did not as yet exist at that time. And he also meant only matters temporal which do not conflict with the commandments of God. The Christian is permitted to resist an unjust order of the authorities.

Therefore I do not reject temporal power altogether, says Chelčický in his *Net of the Faith*, because it directs the whole world in temporal matters to prevent it from downfall. But the Christian should not directly participate in it. Beginning with Constantine, the world belongs to the pagans, while the Christians since then are and always will be an insignificant minority in it.

Not all Chelčický's ideas are new, but his systematic imagination of how the Christian world should be arranged is certainly not lacking in originality. Some things he undoubtedly accepted from the Waldensians (the principle of non-resistance). He was also aided by Wyclif, to whom he often appeals either under his real name or under the name of "Mr. Contrary" (why he should have invented this nickname we do not know), and Huss' pamphlets on simony are cited wherever Chelčický criticizes the Pope or the hierarchy.

By his appeal to the Apostolic Church Chelčický mingled with the apostles and became, to the Bohemians at least, the thirteenth apostle. In his printed *Net of the Faith* of the year 1521 the unknown publisher called him a "man virtuous and noble-minded and a saint in the expectation of God," for "although he was not a magister of all the seven arts, he certainly was a fulfiller of the eight benedictions as well as of all divine commandments, being also a true Bohemian doctor, learned in the law of God and never erring from the truth. In him the word of the prophet came true who said : ' Blessed the man whom thou hast taught, O Lord.' "

When Chelčický's ideas opposing bloodshed came to the knowledge of the German historian Bezold, he wrote : " The existence alone of such truly humane thinking during a reign of iron has something beneficial in it." In our own time Chelčický's fame has been revived by Leo Nikolayevich Tolstoy, who grew enthusiastic over Chelčický's idea of non-resistance to evil. In his work *Your Salvation in Yourselves* he wrote about the *Net of the Faith* as follows : " It is in every respect a wonderful book. . . . Not only that it is highly interesting regardless of our point of view, it is also one of the most remarkable fruits of thought not only by the depth of its contents but by the marvellous vigour and beauty of the national tongue as well."

All Chelčický's works, although possessing many evangelical virtues, and voicing the ideas of a Christian who always forgives and never condemns people, but only their thoughts, and who loves even his enemies, are full of sacred fire and great wrath. Hence also the multitude of strong, almost peasant-like, expressions. Eternal justice and the teaching of Christ meant more to him than the State.

What he preached inflamed the soul and put reason and learning to shame. The life of Christ seemed to him to have two qualities ; charitable love and patience. Chelčický is typical of the kind of men produced by Hussitism.

V

The Bohemian Brotherhood

WHEN George, Lord of Poděbrady and leader of the four Hussite counties in the east of Bohemia, took possession of Prague in 1448, and when, a little later, he became Administrator of the Kingdom in the name of the King, the minor, Ladislaus Posthumus, the decline of Hussitism was checked to some extent. It was, nevertheless, great. In Prague alone there were only two parochial priests who could be called genuinely Hussitic. This was the work of the unhappy Compacts. During George's administration the elected Archbishop Rokycana, whom the terrorism of Sigmund's reign had driven into exile, also returned, in 1448, and took possession of his parish of Týn Church. When the decline of Hussitism is spoken of, what is mainly meant is the relaxation of discipline. Rokycana was the first to thunder against this, and it is due chiefly to him that the Calixtine party recovered, regaining also its self-consciousness, although even the boy king showed signs of his hatred of all that savoured of Hussitism. But the dream of an independent Hussite Church in the midst of the Catholic Church vanished when its organization was destroyed by the persistent refusal of Rome to recognize the elected archbishop.

It was for this reason that Rokycana put no restraint upon himself.

During the reign of Ladislaus Posthumus there began the strange journeys of a pious pilgrim through Bohemia. This was *Brother Řehoř* (Gregor). He crossed the country in all directions in search of good priests. Might there not be, somewhere in the land, " good priests," who would, by their pure teaching and immaculate life, assure to pious people a valid partaking of the holy sacraments and a safe communication with God ?

Such priests Brother Řehoř went in search of. The impulse for his undertaking came from Rokycana's sermons. Řehoř himself was from somewhere in Western Bohemia, of the small nobility, but poor. It is said that he was the son of Rokycana's sister. He entered the Prague monastery " Na Slovanech," which at that time was in possession of the Hussites ; its former inmates, the Croatian monks, having been expelled some time previously. Řehoř himself relates that he used to preach there. But he remained a layman and knew little Latin. After 1448 the nephew went to hear the sermons of his uncle, which greatly attracted him. From among Rokycana's audience was evolved, about 1453, a small circle of congenial spirits, who copied out Rokycana's sermons, meditated on them in their circle (probably about 1453 in the Slavonic monastery) and when in doubt went to seek Rokycana's advice. The vehement polemic of the latter against the depraved priests confirmed the members of the circle in their belief that the sacraments administered by a bad priest lost their saving virtue.

Brother Řehoř then wandered all through Bohemia

and found a few circles similar to his own in Prague.
They heard of the " pious Williamites," kept up an
intercourse with them, but were disappointed. They
learnt that the Williamites exacted contributions from
the peasants in respect of their forest holdings, not
being satisfied with tithes and taxes. In addition to
this, their doctrine that man, even while in mortal sin,
should partake of the Lord's Supper, was considered
unfavourable. Priest Martin Lupáč in Chotěbor was
more to Brother Řehoř's liking, being a pious and a
true counsellor. He also became acquainted with the
Táborites, who then had two good priests, Jacob and
Opočen. But they every time went back to Rokycana
who, in their opinion, " conversed most sensibly of all
on the faith of Lord Christ and the Christian life."
About 1455 Rokycana advised his zealots to make the
acquaintance of Peter Chelčický, whose works Rokycana held in great esteem. From Chelčický and his
followers—the Chelčický " brethren "—the Prague
circle gained much information but did not join them,
for, after all, they were seeking " a good priest," and
Peter was no priest.

In the great, busy town, life seemed hard to Brother
Řehoř and his fellows. Therefore they entreated
Rokycana, when George Poděbrad became king in
1458, to obtain for them from the king an asylum on
the domain of Litice in the village of Kunvald in
North-eastern Bohemia. " And he assented and then
many faithful ones gathered in Kunwald, not of the
common people alone, but of the knights and priests
as well, until some even put up buildings. And they
attached themselves to the priest Michal, of the Žam-
berk parish, making use of his services." In all
probability Brother Řehoř knew of priest Michal's

existence prior to the year 1458.   Their parting with
Rokycana was friendly.

Kunvald was then the first of Řehoř's communities.
There are reports that it was sought by many believers
whom Řehoř had either found in his wanderings or
gained over to his ways of thinking.

Another such community was that of the Moravian
Brothers at Klatovy in the Šumava region.   They certainly were strange devotees.   When Brother Řehoř
made their acquaintance, they already had a hard past
behind them.   These Moravians happened to meet
once (about 1450) in Kroměříž before the pulpit of
the priest Štěpán, who, like Rokycana in Prague,
described the depravity of both the population and
clergy.   They stayed there and were banished from
Kroměříž together with him, and two of their society
were cruelly executed : Brother Milena by quartering,
Brother Jeníček by burning at the stake.   Štěpán
and his flock settled in Valašské Meziříčí where, besides Štěpán, a Táborite priest suddenly appeared who
wandered from place to place, secretly administering,
in the " apostolic way," i.e. without vestments, ordinary
bread in earthen dishes and to seated communicants.
But when these devotees were expelled from Meziříčí
(also through the influence of priest Štěpán), they had
to seek a new place of refuge.   They found it at Moravian Krumlov, where they joined the young priest
Beneš, but soon lost him, as he was burnt at the stake
in Brno not long afterwards.   Knowing of no good
priest in Moravia, they wandered as far as Domažlice
in the Šumava region, and from there, after much persecution, to Klatovy.   From Klatovy they were ejected
four times and once kept six months in jail, but in
spite of all this they always managed to return there in

some indirect way. They also had to stand their trial before Rokycana three times, but would not give up their doctrine of the bad priests, against whom they continued to warn people everywhere. Their devotion to their doctrines was remarkable. One of them, Svatoň by name, had both his hands and feet cut off by the people of Klatovy. The only member of the community who was occasionally able to help them was that Brother Paleček who appeared, some time later, at the court of King George as his court jester and " Bohemian philosopher."

Brother Řehoř was instrumental in uniting the Klatovy Moravians with Kunvald, in about 1458 or 1459. We do not know the details, only the basis of the fusion. " Then we agreed," noted Brother Řehoř, " to give up all writings which are contrary to the law of God, and to content ourselves with the Holy Scripture and be directed by the law of God. And what can be defined by the law of God, that we judged to be good and took a liking for, but that which cannot . . . we condemned as being uncertain."

If the search for a good priest and dependence on him could still be called a Catholic view, the biblical basis of all doctrines was already a Protestant principle.

The third Brotherhood community arose in Vitanovice near Mladá Vožice. To explain this it should be stated that after Peter Chelčický's death his followers from Chelčice moved to that place because they found a good priest there and were persuaded to take that step by Brother Řehoř. They were joined there by the members of the former sect of the Nichlasist (Mikulášencŭ), the Košat body which belonged to the " brothers and sisters of the free spirit," and which had been dispersed by Žižka himself.

I am not acquainted in detail with the religions in other European countries, but nevertheless cannot imagine how a religious body like this of Řehoř, which called itself the Union of the Bohemian Brethren, could have been born anywhere else. It was a purely popular religious society, founded on the popular views of piety and faith, with a minimum of theology and dogma. Simply a Church of the people.

Naturally, the Calixtine clergy hurled anathemas at the sight of these apostates, and the Catholics were even more violent. Diversity of views in regard to Christian doctrines was, in the beginning, undoubtedly great, but still greater were the innovations in respect of ceremony. Therefore complaints of the Kunvald people were of daily occurrence at the court of King George and at the palace of Archbishop Rokycana. These complaints were listened to by the King, and especially by the Queen, Johanna. King George stood by the Compacts and declared in his coronation oath that he would not suffer heresy in the country. The Brethren, not coming within the protecting clauses of the Compacts, were, in 1460, suddenly persecuted by the royal authorities, and imprisoned and even tortured. From that period date the Brotherhood's first seven martyrs, among them Jacob Chulava at Vyškov, burnt at the stake by the Archbishop of Olomouc Tas, after three years of jail had failed to break down his convictions. " When they led him to his death, he spoke much that was good and proclaimed his faith. And his wife was there with their two daughters and three sons. Then the officers said to him : ' Dear Jacob, think of thy faithful wife and thy dear and handsome children and do not put them to such shame and grief. Consider well what thou art about to do and have pity on them, for we know thee for a good man.   Only say that a bad priest can do as much as a good one.'   To which Jacob responded : ' Dear sirs ! I beg of you not to desire me to speak against my dear Lord Jesus, for it is He who has said that a bad tree cannot bear good fruit.'   And asking then a moment's grace to say his prayers, he went and ended his life."

Even during this persecution the Brethren concentrated their attention on a thorough organization. Their first care was for the Brotherhood priests, and therefore they studied the other existing Church bodies to see if they could not find instruction there. B. Tůma, " a good Latinist and something of a physician," went on that account through Hungary and the Balkans, and some even wanted to go in search of Christians to the Indies, where perhaps the legendary priest John might be found.   But when they could find no Church independent of Rome to which they could attach themselves, they elected their own priests in 1464 at their prayer-meetings at the village Lhota near Rychnov.   They chose by lot three from nine men known for their religious zeal and had them ordained by a Waldensian priest.   One of them, Brother Matthei, a peasant from Kunwald, about 25 years of age, was recognized as bishop.

Within twenty years of its settling at Kunvald, the Brotherhood spread out greatly both over Bohemia and Moravia and embraced all classes of the population ; it comprised priests, Prague students, knights, burghers and, of course, most of the country people.

Then began the inner ferment, caused chiefly by the people of learning who had joined the Brotherhood, but that ferment had spent its force in the last

decade of the fifteenth century. The dispute lay
between the original primitiveness of the Brotherhood and the spirit of progress, a dispute of the old
Brethren from the country with the new Brethren,
among whom there were men just as pious as the
original founders, but scholarly as well (Klenovský),
former Calixtine and Táborite clergymen, bachelors
of arts, and aristocrats. These men were being led
into the Brotherhood by the lamentable conditions in
the Utraquist Church and by the moral sincerity they
observed in the Brethren. They put their erudition
at the service of the Brotherhood. Among the old
unlearned majority, however, there were many who
feared that the intellectuals would spoil the Church by
their theological knowledge. These old believers
were called the " little party," while the " great party "
grew from the new and educated members, led by
Brother Lucas of Prague, a former bachelor of arts.
When he came to know the Brethren well he sold all
he had and went to buy a new field with a hidden
treasure. With him went his brother, a famous
physician, John called Černý (Black). This was
about 1490. At the end of the century the Brotherhood abandoned many of Chelčický's principles and
accepted a new and less rigid course, especially in
regard to temporal power. They agreed that " lords
or officials, councilmen or magistrates, who hold their
positions for good reasons and cannot give them up,
when they use their authority correctly and in such
manner as it was instituted for that end by God, such
shall be given a place among us." It was also agreed
that to take an oath was permissible and that military
service was not to be condemned unconditionally as
conflicting with Christianity ; a Brother can participate

in a just war, waged in defence of the country or of right. Against the " little party " in the Brotherhood the principle of the advantage of education was also accepted. The beginning of the sixteenth century already marks the complete victory of this idea, although even Brother Lucas (who died in 1528) did not look on higher education with any special favour.

For the main seat of the Brotherhood the town of Mladá Boleslav was selected by Brother Lucas. He may be considered the second founder of the Brotherhood, because he gave it a new spirit as well as a new organization and defended it against all sorts of enemies by an immense number of works and treatises. After the death of the first bishop Matěj (Mathew) four bishops were elected, two for Bohemia and two for Moravia, so as to make autocracy on the part of one bishop impossible. From the circles of the Brethren scattered all over the country new congregations were formed. And before long the Brotherhood prospered to such an extent—in face of its persecution by both the Kings of the Polish dynasty —that the greatest lords of the country either became directly members of the Brotherhood or at least its patrons and protectors. At the beginning of the sixteenth century there can be named Bohuš Kostka of Postupice in the Litomyšl country, Jan of Žerotín, Jan Tovačovský of Cimburk in the Mladá Boleslav country, Jan of Šelmberk, etc., but the chief place among them was held by the famous Vilém of Pernštejn, whose enormous estates were literally strewn over with Brotherhood communities. From the year 1480 the Brotherhood also had some German congregations. The Brethren brought a number of the persecuted Waldensians from Brandenburg to Moravia, and settled them near Fulnek and Lanškroun after they had accepted the doctrines and regulations of the Brotherhood.

Even if the Brotherhood had lost, in Brother Lucas' time, some of its original rusticity, we need not regret it, for it had gained, on the other hand, many men prominent in learning, or powerful on account of their estates, so that without them it could hardly have attained its later fame, if it had been at all able to withstand the oppression from all sides, especially that of the Habsburgs, who, in 1526, came to occupy the Bohemian throne.

We often find, even in Bohemian literature, the Brethren reproached with their passivity in matters temporal, a passivity which was thought to constitute a danger to the nation, especially the doctrine of non-resistance. This is a mistake. The Brotherhood gave up its principle of opposition to war, and that it knew how to resist evil was seen in the reign of the first Habsburg. The Brethren were not Quakers. It was shown, both under the two Poles and Ferdinand I, that the Catholic party were not mistaken in considering the Brotherhood a stronghold of Bohemian heresy. Therefore it leagued itself, in the diets as well as secretly, with both the deluded Utraquists and the Lutherans against the Pikards and incited the sovereign against them.

When the Habsburgs took possession of the Bohemian throne, the Calixtines naturally suffered. The first Habsburg finally obtained the ratification of the Compacts, that is, after the Calixtines no longer cared for them as having been nothing but a halter around their necks for over a century. Ferdinand I needed the Compacts for his Machiavellian policy, which aimed at getting the remaining handful of the old Calixtines into his power in order to make willing instruments of them for the suppression of the heretics throughout the whole country. At that period these orthodox Calixtines did not differ, properly speaking, from the Catholics in anything but the use of the chalice, certainly not in essentials or dogmas, while the great majority of the Calixtines had already accepted the principles of Luther and would have nothing to do with Rome at all. But the Brethren, standing, as they did, outside the pale of the law, fared much worse. An insignificant Catholic minority among the so-called Estates occupied, through the influence of the court, all the highest offices in the kingdom. And the prevailing opinion of Rome, as expressed in the year 1500 by Alexander VI, that infamous man who was a disgrace to the Church, was that heretics must be belaboured with two hammers, teaching and temporal power, in order to destroy them. In their blindness the Calixtines did not realize, when offering the King an axe to be used against the Brothers, that this very axe was about to be sharpened against themselves.

True, Ferdinand I feared nobody so much as the Brotherhood, and this fear was inherited from him by all Habsburgs, despite the fact that the Brotherhood was a community of moderates, who united for " leading, through the spirit of love, a virtuous life, peaceful, quiet, abstemious, patient, pure. . . ." This Ferdinand I found out immediately after the rebellion of the Estates against him in 1547, which, unfortunately, failed.

The King revenged himself for the rebellion on the towns, and the Brethren by confiscating the estates of the Brotherhood nobility, by enslaving the towns and by driving the common people into exile. But all persecution was in vain. On the contrary, the Brotherhood became the very hearth of national culture.

VI

Bishop Jan Blahoslav

UNDER Brother Lucas the Brotherhood emerged from its infancy ; after that its inner development was gratifying. It became reconciled " with the world," took charge of the schools, arts and science and was not averse to participating in temporal offices.

While Brother Lucas was yet active as a man of mature age, a successor and continuer of his work was already growing up. This was Jan Blahoslav, who was born in 1523, at Přerov in Moravia, and was not only born, but also brought up, in a pure Brotherhood family, which, although noble, was not rich, but inspired by higher interests. This is shown by the fact that the Blažek family presented the Brotherhood with well-educated sons, our Blahoslav and his younger brother Martin Abdon. At Přerov Blahoslav grew up under the eyes of an eminent priest, Brother Volf. When Blahoslav reached his seventeenth year, Volf sent him to Prostějov, to the famous house of the Brotherhood there and the " Community " of another excellent man, Brother Michalec. Three years afterwards he was at school in Germany, at Goldberg and Wittenberg (where he heard Luther preach occasionally). After returning home he stayed for some

149

time with the famous Brother Strejc and Čermák and in 1549 again went to study at Koenigsberg in Germany and Basle in Switzerland ; in this latter place he had the privilege of a friendly intercourse with the humanitarian Sigmund of Jelení. He was already 30 years old when he became a deacon of the Brotherhood (1552) and priest. In Mladá Boleslav he assisted Brother Černý in the archives.

Blahoslav never became a learned theologian. For, coming of the moderate Melanchthon party, he refrained from the " fury of the theologians." And yet his achievements for the Brotherhood were magnificent. He was its historian, founding the Brotherhood Archive, the fifteen volumes of which became one of the jewels of Bohemian literature. He himself wrote a brief history of the Brotherhood and some smaller historical treatises.

Blahoslav was also the Brotherhood's guardian and publicist and that from the moment when he was sent by the elders to Mladá Boleslav, where the famous Mount Carmel congregation was just about to be closed (in 1548), after the unhappy rebellion of the Bohemian Estates against Ferdinand I. Blahoslav then elaborated for the knight Arnošt Krajíř the first of the series of those defensive letters of the Brotherhood which, together with the many diplomatic journeys in the interest of the Brotherhood to foreign countries (to Vienna, Wittenberg, etc.), afterwards became his life's work. He was the chariot-driver, holding the Brotherhood by the reins or curbing it so as to keep the road and not be led into ravines or blind alleys, where it would lose its pure popular and Bohemian originality, as the pious foundation of Bohemian Christianity. For Blahoslav's time was a time of

anxieties, of persecutions by Ferdinand I and denun-
ciations by the Calixtines ; some of the Brethren
hoped that the Brotherhood would be strengthened by
uniting with the Lutherans, while, in its very bosom,
Bishop Augusta, recently discharged from prison and
immensely popular on account of his sufferings, began
to avail himself of demagogy against the men of
erudition.   Let us pause a moment at this incident so
as to understand what it meant to Blahoslav.   This
hatred of the Muses, a thing so disagreeable, exasperated him as " almost to break his heart," as he
wrote of himself.   Three days afterwards (August
15th to 18th 1567) he wrote an answer, in a shaky,
all but illegible, hand, owing to his terrible excitement.
It is recorded in the Brotherhood's Archives and we
know it in printed form as the *Philippic against the
Enemies of Higher Education in the Brotherhood*.   That
philippic was a flaming sword, the blows of which
meant death to erroneous doctrines.   " Youth should
learn ! " said Blahoslav.   " They should learn when
and wherever they find anything good.   For example.
A precious stone or a pearl, artistically and skilfully
cut and polished—how it differs from one which is
neither cut nor polished.   Likewise, an axe, just made
but not yet sharpened or smoothed.   And what would
a sword be like, unsharpened and unmeasured. . . .
He that despises learning and art resembles him that
would make clothes for himself or others, but would
know nothing of the tailoring trade, would refuse to
learn and also abuse and vilify it. . . ."   Thus, Blahoslav
was a historian and a publicist, I am almost tempted to
say that he was the journalist, of the Brotherhood.
Either capacity would have gained fame for him
in our history, for whatever he did, he did excellently.

But, first of all, Blahoslav was a poet and a musician, the greatest of his time in Bohemia, and what he has accomplished with these talents of his can never be valued sufficiently. Blahoslav's poetical gifts appeared in his first two works. In 1550 he wrote—being then 27 years of age—an *Essay on Eye-sight, how man can by his eye-sight, i.e. by seeing and looking, harm either himself or other*. In the same year—1550—he collected evidence about holy (and other) persons of the clerical profession, who either became prominent in the Brotherhood from its beginning or had laboured for it. These were short necrologies, which characterized old characters according to what Blahoslav used to hear from aged men or as he came to learn them himself. This collection is called the *Mortality Book*, although the still preserved lengthy title reads : " In this book may be found the happy ending of lives and a delightful decease in our Lord of many persons, etc."

Anyone who has ever touched these two works must have noticed that their contents are really delightful. The work on eye-sight is not a mere treatise ; there are paragraphs in it which could have been penned by nobody but a poet, and paragraphs evincing great gifts of observation, particularly so in the deep impressions nature has made on the author, an unusual feature in a man of the sixteenth century. The *Mortality Book* again excels in its acute, concise and really plastic descriptions, as if the characters had been chiselled out of rock. He who possesses the divine gift of observation and also the art of depicting his impressions to the reader exactly as he received them, is a real poet. This poetical gift of Blahoslav was supported and perfected by much musing upon the Bohemian language. Later he confesses in his Grammar, that the Czech language he " cherishes with an extraordinary love."

These poetical talents, as well as his love of the Czech language, were placed by Blahoslav at the service of the Brotherhood and the service of God, just as everything else that he had and knew. He was never in doubt, never stood at the crossroads between worldly fame and the clerical profession. And it is in this that the piety of a true Bohemian Brother appears to great advantage. Blahoslav did not serve the Brotherhood as a learned theologian in mere dogmatical disputes, yet he effected more for the purity of religion than all his famous contemporaries together. He did great service to pure religion by his beautiful, penetrating and noble works, such as the translation of the New Testament and *Samotul Cantionale* (hymn-book). It seemed as if his whole life's effort were directed at making the word of God and the devotional songs beautiful. "For he who considers the Scriptures as divine teachings, can neither read nor explain them otherwise than with the most perfect speech of which man is capable. He who desires to sing praise of God worthily may not keep the church song on the mere level of secular song, but will ever select both words and melody of the most sacred type." To this service Blahoslav devoted himself with all his heart, and a person more competent than he certainly did not then exist. He was a poet born and in song and music he diligently trained himself. He knew much secular song and loved to sing ; in his Grammar he mentions how they used to sing in the house of Zikmund of Jeleni at Basle where he also wrote out his Croatian ballads. Strew a flowering green with stone—the blossoms will break through and shoot up between it.

No occupation could stifle in Blahoslav the blossoms
of his spirit—whether he composed his polemical
treatises, wrote his grammar, or scourged the faults of
the preachers. His poesy bloomed so much freer
when he translated tender or profound evangelical
parables or composed religious songs for the pious
Brethren. So powerfully does Blahoslav's poetical
talent penetrate to the surface, that I would unhesi-
tatingly call him the poet of the sixteenth century,
although he never wrote either poems or any other
fiction.

In 1561 the *Kancionál bratrský* (Brotherhood
Hymnal), composed and arranged by Blahoslav, was
published. It is called Šamotulský, because it was
printed in Šamotul in Poland. At Ivančice again, in
1564, appeared the New Testament, which Blahoslav
translated from the Greek original.

These are the two pillars of Bohemian literature and
Bohemian music on which our literary and musical
structure still rests. Or, better expressed, two sources,
giving the water of life to both the healthy and the
sick ; to those who had to be yet born as well as to
those who had already partaken of their delights and
were dying ; two sources from which we drink to this
day. Blahoslav intended them to be of service to the
Brotherhood and by so doing performed an inestimable
service to the whole nation, to his contemporaries,
and still more to his descendants. The blessing of
the Reformation was and still is the fact that in all the
nations where it took hold, it not only strengthened
the religious spirit but also laid the foundations of
nationality and of national culture. From these books
the nation drew its religious enthusiasm, not only
because of their piety but also because they were beau-

tiful, touching with their lingual and musical delights the tenderest feelings of the soul. There was a time in which the strength of these healing sources was recognized even by the Jesuits, and that was when the nation was perishing before their very eyes. The Jesuit Steyer recommended, at the end of the seventeenth century, in his book *To the Little Scholar*, that Catholics should learn good language from the Bible Králická (a Bible printed at Králiky, Bohemia, into which Blahoslav's New Testament was incorporated), and the same Jesuit took, for his Catholic hymnal, many hymns from the *Samotul Cantionale*, four written by Blahoslav among them ; of course, not forgetting to catholicize them as far as possible.

Wherever these two books were preserved, whether by the Bohemian people at home or by those in exile, there the national treasure was also preserved in its original purity until the advent of the better days, until our national " awakening " at the end of the eighteenth century. On the other hand, where, through the influence of the Jesuit schools, hatred against either the Králická Bible or the Brotherhood Cantional took root, there also arose (knowingly and spitefully in the case of many persons) a new Bohemian, the so-called " Language of St. Venceslaus," which perished miserably in the notorious Pohl's Grammar of the Joseph II era and in the musical freak known as Fryčaj's Catholic Cantional. It was a great piece of fortune for the nation that after translating the Scriptures the poet made use of his real talent and great linguistic taste. Blahoslav's inner fire was so intense that it heated even the coldest matter. His pupils finished the Scriptures entirely in his spirit. According to experts, the Bohemian is the most poetical of all the European translations of the Bible. The names of the translators we know, but to our regret not the name of the artist who executed the ornamental part of the *Králická Bible*. If Blahoslav personified both the poet and musician, the artist who illuminated it represented the nucleus of the future national art, which, unfortunately, after 1620 could not mature. The Catholic writers would like to depict the Brothers as Trappists or Quakers, as hypocritical enemies of life with its beauties and joys. But against this stands, as a beautiful witness, the figure of Blahoslav.

We may say that the Brotherhood was at its best when it gave to the world the *Králická Bible*, not as a translation alone, but also with commentaries, which show us the Bohemian religious doctrines in their purest form. Although it differs from both Luther and Calvin, the *Králická Bible* is on that very account truly native, typical Bohemian, and therefore the most satisfying to Huss' descendants.

Then there are two other memorable works by Blahoslav : the *Musika*, published at Olmutz in 1558, and the *Gramatika česká* (Bohemian Grammar), completed in the year of his death in 1571, but not issued in print till 1857. Yet let nobody be misled by the dating. These works are the accompaniments of the Cantional and the New Testament. The *Musika* is only a partial theory of music, although, in the opinion of experts, an excellent work in itself, and the Grammar is not a grammar book in our sense of the word, not even a "whetstone," as works of this kind are sometimes called, but just a line of theoretical explanations, reasons and proofs, why Blahoslav used, in the New Testament, such and such words, such and such

phrases, and why he rejected, in the older translations
as well as in the teachings of some grammarians, certain, in his opinion, gross errors against the spirit of
the language and especially the vulgar words and
phrases used there.   The *Gramatika* in particular is a
delightful production of Blahoslav's intellect, the
material for which he was engaged in collecting nearly
all his life.   It is strewn over with a multitude of real
pearls.   There are many comments on the older
orators and writers, regular literary historical excur-
sions, as well as anecdotes, recollections of people both
native and foreign, dialectal observations and altogether a great part of Blahoslav's intimate biography,
so that this Grammar—Grammar !—reads like a
delightful itinerary, full of pleasantness and sparkling
wit.   The same can be said of the *Musika*, although a
book of very small size.

Blahoslav closed his Grammar with a touching
epilogue as if parting with his life work.   " I desired
to help our tongue *ad veram tum puritatem tum ornatem.*
And this I desired so earnestly that my mind often
burned like a kindled torch.   Nor would it leave me
in peace, although I often tried to choke and put it out
of my mind by considering : (1) my incapacity, which,
I thought, would prevent me from accomplishing
much.   (2) The lack of time . . . etc.   But then
again other things cheered me and even commanded
that I should steal some of my time from myself for
the writing of these grammatical things.   Only I
could not remain as long at the reading and diligent
judging of *authorum theologicorum* as I would have
liked to, for my eyes were growing faint, as also my
head.   (3) Often, being tired and all worn out, I ran
away as if *ad leviora studia, a literis velut a scorpionibus,*

ut Erasmus inquit, remedium patens. (4) *Scribere prav-
iora, sempe theologica supra vires mens videbatur,* and
also (*Ut verum fatear*), when I could, I did not want
to and when I was willing, I could not. . . . And
I have nothing more to add to this, but that I turn to
Thee, O Lord, that if these labours of mine, of which
there were not a few, should, with all that frippery and
stubble, be burnt (as, undoubtedly, many parts of them
will), then, pray, only pardon my want of sense and do
with me merely what it pleased Thy spirit to say, which
is, that I should be saved and preserved to Thee, with
Thee and Thy saints for all eternity. And were I called
to pass through the fire, even that I shall and do accept,
if it will only with Thy help, lead directly to a good end.
Amen. Amen."

Not long after this confession Blahoslav died. The
Brethren undoubtedly reminded themselves later of
many words in that " conclusion," such as the weak
eye-sight and headache ; how often this great man
must have been tired and almost worn out, what an
amount of work he had to perform. But they scarcely
believed that his labours—frippery and stubble as he
called them—had been in vain. I need not enumerate
all the works written by Blahoslav, there being about
fifty of them, yet it is necessary to mention one more,
the *Vady Kazatelů*, a work as full of hints and sparks of
intellect as of masterly pictures. He wrote this work
at the request of his friends, and also because he
thought that as a bishop he should be, in word and
deed, an example to the younger preachers. " And
because I cannot preach before them in the Lord's
congregations on account of my poor health, I wish
this writing may compensate therefor to some extent."

Respect for the worth of Blahoslav's works will not

increase owing to the circumstances of his life, but
esteem for the man himself must rise to admiration
when I remind the reader that Blahoslav's complaints
about his poor health were not mere verbal embellish-
ment. The man was ailing for the greater part of his
life. The first time he fell seriously ill was at Basle
in 1549 ; he lay there all through the winter and was
not allowed to return to Přerov till after Easter. In the
year when he was elected archbishop (1557) and had
to go on missions to the Vienna court, his journeys
were also connected with the desire for medical help
from Dr. Kraton in Vienna. Blahoslav's friend B. Nik-
odem had to journey as far as Venice for medicines
for the bishop. In the same year (1567) Blahoslav
spent some time in Vienna for treatment, and already,
in 1568, again complained to Dr. Kraton that his
health was deplorable. From September 5th 1571 he
suffered so intensely with fever that he could not even
participate in the Synod of the Elders, although it
was held at Ivančice, his own seat. At this time he
was tormented by his last great anxiety—the desire to
see his Confession and the History of the Brotherhood
finished in Latin for foreigners. Yet in spite of that
he went in November on an episcopal visitation to
Mor. Krumlov and there, on November 24th, was
called away by death. Knowing all this we are
amazed ; for how could this man in the midst of the
din of arms, the noise of religious troubles, in the
midst of political journeys and episcopal duties suffering agues and fever that consumed his body, how
could this man perform works of such rare merit ?
And all this was accomplished in the short term of
48 years. One, at least, of Blahoslav's peculiarities
we shall easily comprehend—the brevity of his style

and the frequent premisses concluded with numberless
" etceteras," which are a sign of how hurriedly and
feverishly he worked.   He never had time to express
himself fully, to finish his sketch drawing.   This
haste also is undoubtedly responsible for his incessant
passing over from Czech to Latin and from Latin to
Czech again.   His memory was full of quotations
from Latin writers, theologians and poets ; having
no time to translate or to seek a Bohemian term (our
terminology, whether poetical, grammatic or musical
being then in its infancy) he shook out as it were from
his sleeve what was ready.   To us moderns much in
his work may sound unpleasant, but it is only just to
acknowledge that no writer of his time worked under
greater handicaps than he, for none of them wrote of
things as novel as he.

No wonder then, that Blahoslav's name had " great
fame throughout the nation," or that he was acquainted
personally with nearly all the European reformers of
his time.   Melanchthon, it seems, he personally liked
the best.   The Brotherhood must have known his
worth, when it gave him, then only 34 years of age, a
place among their bishops.   The Moravian provincial
marshal, the Lord of Lipé and an antagonist of the
Brotherhood, when conversing in Vienna with the
court-physician Dr. Kraton, asked him :   " What do
you think of Jan Blahoslav.   Is he a learned man ? "
Kraton's categoric answer was : " In my opinion you
have no man more learned in all Bohemia or Moravia."
The marshal : " That is what I have heard of him."

We understand therefore the grief felt by the
Brotherhood when, on November 24th 1571, Bishop
Jan Blahoslav died.   " A father and leader of all the
Lord's people in the Brotherhood, a great and remark-

THE TYN CHURCH, PRAGUE.

[To face p. 160

able man, very pious, industrious from his youth, kind to all, whose fame was carried far among other peoples. A great and precious jewel of the Brotherhood ; all too soon, in our judgment, did it please the Lord God to take him away from our midst." Thus reads the record of him by Brother Vavřinec Orlík, his friend and the continuer of the *Mortality Book*, begun by Blahoslav.

In our age Blahoslav has no longer the wide fame among the nations that he had, for the world is now larger than it was in the sixteenth century. But to our nation he is the same precious jewel to-day as he was in his time to the Brotherhood, and even dearer perhaps, because we can appreciate the splendid qualities of his character as well as his stupendous life-work, an appreciation of which his contemporaries were not always capable. And, above all else, his language is to us like tablets on which the laws of the Czech tongue made sacred and beautiful to the nation by him are indelibly written.

In studying Bohemian Hussitism and the Brotherhood, the query naturally forces itself upon us—would it not be possible to talk of *national* churches too ? Christianity, as contained in the Bible, is certainly the same for all nations, but the people are not alike. For it is possible to point to the fact that the churches which originated among the Slavonic nations from the Luther and Calvin reformations, all furnished a basis for national literature. This the Bohemians discovered the best in themselves : Hussitism, like the Brotherhood, is the highest Bohemian expression of the national spirit. The same can also be said in regard to the Poles, and the very first book the Slovenes knew was Protestant (Primož-Trubar). In our time Catholic zealots often try to intimidate the Bohemian people with explanations that the Bohemians would surely have been Germanized if it had not been for the Battle of the White Mountain and the defeat of Protestantism, because Protestantism was German. What sense there is in this Catholic patriotic philosophy is hard to understand. History itself speaks against it eloquently. In the first place, the Bohemians had their own Reformation as early as the fifteenth century—a reformation which was anti-German, not German. Nor was the reformation of the sixteenth century German, for Calvin was French. That the Germanization of the Bohemians was due to Protestantism is mere phantasy ; that it was brought about, however, after the White Mountain by Catholicism is a fact proved by history. After the lapse of 150 years from the Battle of the White Mountain there existed neither a Bohemian literary language in the Bohemian countries nor Bohemian self-consciousness. The Bohemian nationality existed only, and that feebly enough, among the ignorant peasants and inhabitants of the small towns, precisely in such classes of the populace as lacked school education. In striking contrast to this, the Bohemian exiles scattered all over Germany were still reading the Králická Bible and the works of Huss and Komenský.

VII

John Amos Komenský and the Decline of the Brotherhood

BETWEEN Blahoslav and the last Bishop of his Church, Komenský (Comenius), there is a space of fifty years. Blahoslav was the bishop of the Brotherhood when it rose to the summit of its development and glory, while Komenský was its bishop after the catastrophe of the White Mountain. This catastrophe was brought about by the Habsburgs and Rome, whose executive arm in Bohemia was the Jesuits and the Spanish Mission. Ferdinand I obtained the recognition of the Compacts by the Pope with the sole view of extirpating with their help the New Utraquists, as the Lutheran Calixtines were then called. At the same time he filled the archbishopric in Prague with a Catholic and called, in 1556, the Society of Jesus to Bohemia. Only twelve of the Jesuits came at first, with downcast eyes and trembling with fear, for the parting admonition of Pope Paul IV to them had been : " Behold, I send you like lambs into the company of wolves ! "

The Estates had had to fight for their religious liberty for more than 100 years, although they had only one-tenth of the Catholics against them. Finally they had succeeded in extorting from King Rudolph II, in 1609, the so-called Letter of Majesty, which guaranteed religious liberty to Protestants of all denominations. But even this Letter of Majesty was subverted by the intrigues of the so-called Jesuit-Spanish party who, in 1618, drove the Bohemian nobility into an unpremeditated revolution. The revolution was defeated on November 8th 1620 at the White Mountain near Prague.

The victor, Ferdinand II, declared he would rather have the Bohemian Kingdom desolate than heretic. He therefore permitted it to be ravaged as if it were an enemy's country conquered by the sword. He issued orders for the execution of the leaders of the rebellion, and on June 21st 1621, in the Old Town Square in Prague, twenty-seven nobles were executed. He also issued orders to confiscate the estates of the heretics and banished from the country all those who refused to accept the Catholic faith.

In the opinion of the State archivist, Gindely, no greater change than now had ever taken place in Bohemia since the migration of the nations. Regarding the changes of ownership after the White Mountain we have a book of two volumes by Tomáš V. Bílek, *The History of Confiscation in Bohemia after the Year* 1618. The work was published in 1882. It was taken as a model for a list, at least partial, of the confiscation in Moravia and Silesia.

Probably no other Christian nation in Europe has a book like it. If there ever was one with any resemblance to it it can only be the famous Domesday Book of English history, that inventory of the estates of the Anglo-Saxon nobility compiled by the order of William the Conqueror who, after the Battle of Hast-

ings, confiscated the estates of the Anglo-Saxon
nobility and distributed them among the new Norman
lords. Bílek's book looks like a dictionary. The
first 946 pages contain an alphabetical index of the
noble families whose lands were taken by Ferdinand II
either wholly or in part. On pages 947 to 1278
follows the list of the Bohemian towns subjected to the
same treatment ; some of them being wholly reduced
to beggary. The end of the book, from pages 1278
to 1468, is filled with a register of persons and things.
The Balkan Slavs could have produced a similar list
when, in the fifteenth century, they were subjugated
by the Turks.

Bílek has not elaborated this list of confiscated Bohemian property scientifically, but the material of his
book is precious even as it is. For he got hold of it
accidentally and worked it up almost by stealth.
Having been, for his patriotic sentiments, prematurely
deprived of his position as Headmaster of a Bohemian
gymnasium (Grammar School), he spent his leisure in
the governor's library, the officials of which saw no
reason for hindering him in his supposed dilettantism.
There he came, probably by mere chance, across " 103
volumes," each of which contained several hundred
different documents. These proved to be the lists of
the confiscated Bohemian property, kept originally
underground, in a tomb of the former Jesuit Church
of St. Nicholas in the district of Prague known as
the Mala Strana. For a long time these Habsburg
archives were inaccessible to investigators, the keys to it
being in the keeping of an ordinary governor's regis-
trar, and therefore not kept in the customary manner.
The piles of paper, parchment and books lay simply
in wooden partitions, without anybody knowing any-

thing of their contents.   And it was even impossible
to order them properly because the deep vault was
lighted only by small grated windows not unlike a
prison.   When at last, in response to the urgent
requests of the Bohemian diet, a special department
with three officials was established for these archives
in the Governor's building, everything was carried out
in a shabby manner, because the Government acted
only under compulsion and therefore with distaste.
The officials—specially educated historians from
Prague University—could enter the tomb only with
an enormous mediæval lantern weighing many pounds.
They brought up bundle after bundle to our worthy
Bílek, who spent several years copying them out.   In
winter-time he used to sit in a corner of the office clad
in a fur coat and heavy boots, and wrote by the light of
a candle.   But when he later published the result of
his labours, the effect on the Bohemian public was
stupendous, while Austrian officialdom was thunder-
struck.   What sort of stew was this that the old, seem-
ingly inoffensive, pensioner had prepared for them ?
The Bohemian nation suddenly found out from Bílek
that " nearly three-fourths of this kingdom had been
confiscated," possessions worth millions and millions,
that confiscation had meant a change in the country
terrible to contemplate, for the new owners of these
confiscated lands were foreigners, international adventurers, nothing more.   The Emperor bestowed the
estates on his creatures and creditors such as the
Slavates, Martinices, Lobkovices and Waldsteins, of
the natives ; like the Huertas, Marradases, Picco-
lominis, Sporks, Gallases and Colloredos, Desfours,
Aldringens, etc., of the foreigners.   For example,
Count Piccolomini, for assisting in the murder of

Albrecht of Waldstein (Wallenstein) was rewarded with the domain of Náchod and the estate Miskolezy. Colonel Walter Butler was, for the same service, made a count and received the former Waldstein domains, Doksy with Bezděz, Pernstein and Deštná. Don Martin Huerta, once a tailor in his native country, then a lackey and a spy, was made a peer. And so that all those who took part in the rebellion against the Emperor could be the more easily apprehended, " the informers were promised a third." How many of the peasant folks took up this infamous trade ! how many weaklings became scoundrels !

In face of the perpetual danger threatening from the Protestant faction, the sovereign and the nobility were bound together by strong ties of common interests. Obedience and mutual help, which have always been among the laws of feudalism, had to be reaffirmed in the Bohemian countries, where there was especial need of them. The third in the league was the Roman Church ; this again sanctified the bargain and oiled the machinery. Although the main attack was directed against religion, its support, the language, did not escape. The Czech language, as an organ of the intellectual life of the nation, became gradually subordinated to German, until, about the year 1700, the Bohemian nobility were completely denationalized, so that the greater part of the country—the so-called German territory—was settled with Germans ; until there was no literary man in the country who would have dared to write a book in the correct Czech of the Králická Bible. It was a decay intellectual as well as material ; the people were brutalized and without school education. This was the saddest period of all Bohemian history.

After the Battle of the White Mountain it was only in exile that the Czech nation existed. Whatever was then written in Czech and has any literary value, was produced by the exiles. The literary history of that period knows three names : the exile Pavel Skála of Zhoře, Pavel Stránský and John Amos Komenský.

Komenský was a Moravian Slovak from Uherský Brod. He was born on March 28th 1592. After the premature death of his father, a miller, the guardians of the orphaned John did not pay much attention to him. It was some time before he could enter the Brotherhood school at Strážnice. Theology he studied in Herborn and Heidelberg, and on his return became first a teacher at Přerov, then a pastor at Fulnek. His domestic life was also happy (he married in 1618). But Fulnek, too, was to feel the aftermath of the White Mountain battle. It was burnt and devastated by the Spanish troops ; Komenský lost all his property, his library in particular, on that occasion, and soon after was banished from both the town and country. From 1621 to 1627 he remained in hiding with some of the powerful Brotherhood nobles. When staying with Karel Žerotín at Brandýs on the Orlice, he wrote a delightful book, the well-known *Labyrint světa and Raj srdce* (The Labyrinth of the World and the Paradise of the Heart). In concealment on the estate of the knight of Sádovský near the sources of the River Elbe, he occupied himself with pedagogic literature. The year 1627 brought to the Bohemians a *Restored Country Organization* (absolutism) and the Banishing Decree of July 31st. Komenský left his country in 1628 and, it seems, never saw it again.

His exile lasted forty-two years.

Misfortune after misfortune, ill success and losses

continued to heap themselves upon Komenský's head. At first he lived in the Polish town of Lešno, where he turned " again to the dust of the school," i.e., taught the school and employed himself in making outlines for great educational works to be composed later. In 1641 he was invited by the English Parliament to London, the English nation desiring to entrust Komenský with the reform of its schools, but both the journey and his stay in London (1641–1642) had no result, owing to the war with Ireland and the following civil war, which ended in the execution of King Charles I. " The report of the Irish revolt and killing of more than 200,000 Englishmen in one night, the sudden departure of the King from London, as well as the unmistakable signs that a bloody war was near, upset all these plans and compelled me to return in all haste to my family." While Komenský was yet in England up to the end of August 1642, he was invited to France by the learned Mersenne, the friend of Descartes, but preferred the kind invitation of Monsieur Luis de Geer. This latter was a French merchant who, as a Huguenot, had had to seek refuge in Holland. But, being rich, he liberally supported men of science and writers ; Komenský calls him the " Great Almoner of Europe." Geer then lived at Norkeeping in Sweden, from where he wrote to invite Komenský to come to live in his Swedish house, offering him besides financial help that would enable him to work on his philosophical writings. In the meantime the powerful Chancellor of Sweden succeeded in persuading Komenský to make the journey to Sweden (in 1642), for the purpose of reforming the school system there, especially the Latin schools. And should he not want to remove his family to Sweden too, then at least to settle somewhere near. When M. Geer also approved of this idea, Komenský moved to the Prussian town of Elbing, where he devoted himself for six years to school problems. In 1648, having been elected bishop of the Brotherhood, Komenský saw himself compelled to return to Lešno. The Brotherhood lived at that time in exile with Lešno as its central point, the Brothers having begun to emigrate there after 1548, when they were banished from Bohemia for the first time. From an insignificant little place Lešno grew in the period following the battle of the White Mountain to a considerable town, where the Bohemian Brethren formed the majority of the population. The town was held by the noble Polish family of Leščinský and its then living chief was himself a member of the Brotherhood. The main church in the town also belonged to the Brethren. They soon had to let Komenský depart for Hungary, where Prince Rakoczy needed his services as the Swedes had before. In 1650 therefore he removed to Šaryšský Potok, taking his family with him. There he laboured four years, organized, according to his plan, the Pansophic school, but struggled in vain against all kinds of difficulties, of which not the least were the want of discipline among the teachers and the laziness of the pupils. For them he composed the beautifully illustrated work *Orbis Pictus*. Then in 1654, the Church recalled Komenský again, and the Potok school was dispersed by the plague of 1655.

Komenský's third sojourn at Lešno was unfortunate. During the war between Sweden and Poland, the Poles took Lešno, on April 28th 1656, and laid the town in ashes. Komenský lost all his material property and the greater part of his manuscript. As he described it himself : " And there I lost my whole property : my cottage, furniture, library, all my treasures, the fruit of more than forty years of night work and exertion." The hardest blow was the destruction of the large dictionary *Poklad jazyka českého* (Thesaurus linguæ bohemicæ), the material for which he collected from his student days in Herborn. " Never, as long as there is breath in me, will I cease to lament the loss of this work." Komenský fled from the ruined town to Silesia, and the Brotherhood settlement was dispersed all over the various Protestant countries. From Silesia Komenský went to Hamburg, and at Laurence de Geer's invitation, settled permanently in Amsterdam, in 1656. He was then 64 years old. The Netherlands, after their long war of independence, which had lasted since 1609, was a strong support of the Calvinist Reformation and the place of refuge for all the persecuted.

Amsterdam received Komenský with great honour and he lived there in contact with the best people of the country. Four publishing houses competed for the privilege of printing his works. In 1657, at the request of the City Senate, he published his didactical works in three parts and twelve books, known as *J. A. Comenii didactica opera omnia*. He died peaceably in Amsterdam, on November 15th 1670, leaving a son, Daniel, and a daughter, Elizabeth, married to the exile Peter Jablonský. His burial took place a week after his death in the Protestant church near Naarden.

The Jablonský (Figul) family did not become extinct. One of its descendants, Ing. Figulus, was discovered settled in South Africa and after the Great War in 1918 returned to Prague.

On Komenský's death a tombstone was erected to

his memory at Naarden, with an inscription to the effect that Komenský was a "*theologus, didacticus, philosophus.*" Komenský said of himself that he was a Moravian by birth, a Czech by language, and a theologian by profession. As a matter of fact, he sometimes placed his philosophical work above anything else.

Well, then, a theologian! Do not, in the case of Komenský, be scared by the ill-repute attaching to the theologians, of which people were always so much afraid. He was neither a brawler nor a tyrant. The man could not be quarrelsome who wrote : "Therefore I call my brethren all those who invoke the name of Christ, I call my brethren all who are of the same blood, the whole of Adam's descent that inhabits the wide world." Thus speaks a Christian, not a theologian.

When, during the victorious invasion of Bohemia by the Saxon troops, in 1631, the hope flamed up for a moment that Bohemian exiles would be able to return home, Komenský spoke from Lešno. Assuming the garb of that prophet from the Old Testament who, after the return of the Jews from Babylon, began to educate the Jewish people for the restored order of things, he wrote the *Hageus redivivus*. Immediately after he issued his *Didactica*. And in both these books Komenský put propositions of national and political reforms, but in *Hageus* first of all a sketch of the Church reform : "'Ye are brothers, ye are one, what is that you now are doing. . . . Forbear saying : I am of Paul, I of Apollo, I of Huss, I of Luther, I of Calvin ; all of ye, pray, begin to be of Christ and for Christ, not for yourselves ; call together all your disciples and lead them along the easy road of God,

which is called the holy, and entangle them not in con-
troversies from which ye do not know how to dis-
entangle yourselves."

The elements of Komenský's religious tolerance
appear already in his *Labyrinth*. He was always
considered by his contemporaries, but still more so by
posterity, as a pioneer of religious tolerance, and especially a pioneer of the tendency which came later to be
called pietism ; a pioneer of the Irenic ideas, which
desired the world to live in peace and tranquillity.
New principles in that era, indeed ! What was necessary was the reform of life, demanded by Huss and the
leaders of the Brotherhood right from the start ; the
people were to be brought up in practical Christianity.
Therefore the individual creeds should live peaceably
side by side and rather vie with each other in diminish-
ing the evil in the world.

Komenský was, personally, so tolerant of other
Churches, that the Bohemian Jesuit Balbin could not
help admitting : " Komenský would neither give preference to any religion nor repudiate it," and even
that he had written nothing " that would disparage the
Catholic Church in any way." By this Balbin evidently meant the Catholic doctrines, because the
Church *organization* and papal power Komenský never
ceased to combat.

The Brotherhood was, of course, always nearest to
Komenský's heart and he looked after it theologically
if for no other reason than because of his duty as a
Bishop. Sermons, religious exordiums, hymns and
handbooks for believers form the majority of Komenský's works. He also wrote a catechism in German
for the dispersed German Brethren from the neighbourhood of Fulnek. These Brethren finally emi-

grated from Moravia and founded the Restored Brotherhood in Herrnhut (Saxony), in 1720.

Thus Komenský was a theologian in the broad sense of the word ; but a Brotherhood theologian. He tried to reconcile in himself the biblical view with the scientific, accepted the doctrines of Francis Bacon and was personally acquainted with both Descartes and Milton, whose progressive doctrines he absorbed. By this he surpassed, in religious sentiment, the spirit of his time, and anticipated future development. Such are, occasionally, the leaders of mankind. They do not, as a rule, live by the work of others, are not governed by the ideas of their time exclusively : they constantly run ahead of contemporary development and create a new order of things, for which they are often misunderstood by their contemporaries and even repudiated. But future generations bless them.

The progress of Komenský's views as to education and the bringing up of children is enormous in comparison with what he found when he went to school himself.

The ideal of an " educated man " in the seventeenth century was he who knew his Latin and Greek well and who, in imitation of the old authors, wrote fanciful books or composed elegant verses. The indifference to practical education, to a knowledge of nature and natural life in general was incredible. The teachers had accepted this ideal of an " educated man." One of the famous German teachers, Johann Sturm, even suppressed the mother tongue in his school curriculum. Thus as the teachers had altogether a wrong idea of the object of instruction, they naturally chose also wrong means and ways for attaining it. And then there appeared Komenský, who said : " To educate the young does not mean to recite to them, from various books, heaps of words, ways of speaking, the sense of all kinds of phrases, etc., and to stuff them with it ; but to open their intellect, so that as from the bud grow leaves, blossoms and fruit, from it too boughs can grow, and the following year from their buds new boughs again, and so forth until the full growth is reached. And this certainly has been the method of the schools so far. They have not led the young people to the roots of art, but hung them over with boughs torn from books ; they did not stop to uncover the fountain of reason stored in them, but only irrigated them from foreign brooks, which means they did not demonstrate how all things really are in themselves, but how this or another, a third and a tenth describe them ; so that it was considered the greatest art to know what some one else thought and judged them to be. And thus many a student stopping at this point, did not go any farther and even did not know where he should go (for more instruction) ; merely wallowed in books and selecting from them various subjects, ways of speaking and phrases, patched his knowledge together, thus filling his cistern from foreign sources. Horatius, however, seeing all this useless industry, exclaims : ' Oh, ye imitators, ye race of slaves ! A race of slaves ye are, beasts bearing foreign burdens ! For, why should I dress in foreign feathers, having my own ? Why look through other eyes, having my own ? Why reason with another's reason, having reason of my own ? ' "

In another place Komenský says : " Come, let us go out into God's Nature. There you will see all that God created in the beginning and is still creating through Nature. After that we will go to towns, warehouses and schools, where you will see how people turn this divine work to their own benefit and how they educate themselves in art, manners and languages. Then we will enter houses, courts and palaces of princes in order to see in what way human society is directed. Finally we will also visit churches there to see how differently the mortals try to worship their Creator and to communicate with him spiritually and how all things are managed by His omnipotence" (from *The Gate*, 1652, in English).

The Germans and the Jesuits despised the mother tongue most of all. Therefore German remained for long quite clumsy and the learned German preferred to write in Latin, later in French. The Jesuits again did not wish the nations to flourish independently to the detriment of the universality of the Church. Latin was to connect the nations also in their private life in their conversation. The pupils of the higher classes were allowed to speak in their mother tongue only on holidays, while the younger teachers were warned not to read books written in their mother tongue, especially poetry, firstly, so as not to waste time and then not to spoil their morals. Here again Komenský was of another opinion. He says in this respect : " To teach some one a foreign language before he has not his native tongue at his finger-tips, is exactly as if a man would teach his son to ride before he can walk. . . . Let every race be instructed in its own language, so that the youth be not imprisoned in the schools as was, unjustly, done till now from a great contempt for the common people and the national tongues. Thus allow not the study of wisdom to be carried on only in Latin any more.

" Our aim is that all humanity be educated for all

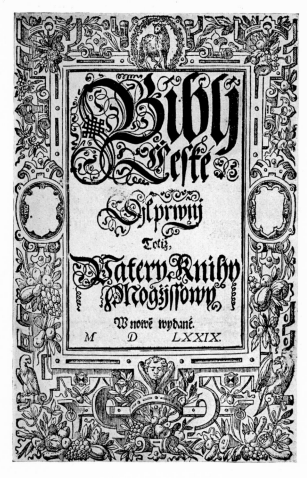

TITLE-PAGE OF EARLY CZECH BIBLE.

[*To face p.* 176

that is human. . . . The aim and goal of the elementary school should be that all the young between their sixth and twelfth or thirteenth year should learn all those things which are useful through their whole life " (Large Didactic). Then follow the details :

" It is not proper that only the children of rich and noble be sent to school, but all without difference, highborn and lowborn, rich and poor, boys and girls in all cities, towns, villages and hamlets. And this because, first, those who were born human, were born mainly for the purpose of becoming human beings, that is, intelligent creatures, the rulers of all creatures who show their resemblance to the Creator.

" Nor is there any sufficient reason why the weaker sex should be kept away from the arts of wisdom entirely. For they, too, are the image of God ; they, too, partake of Grace and the Kingdom to come ; they, too, are gifted with a mind quick to understand and susceptible to wisdom, often more than the male sex. To them, too, the road to high affairs is open, frequently even to the governing of nations ; to giving excellent advice to kings and princes, also to the medical art and other matters beneficial to mankind. . . . Why, then, should we admit them to the alphabet first and drive them from books afterwards. Or are we afraid of their impertinence ? The more we occupy them with ideas, the less room will be in their heads for pertness, which generally is caused by emptiness of mind."

No other older pedagogue evinced so much attention and love for children as did Komenský. His treatise *Informatorium of the Mother School* (1632) is sometimes rightly called " a golden little book of sensible maternal love and care." Komenský set out

M

to prove that the education of a child begins at its most tender age and thus is the business of mothers or parents. This is a booklet of a precious smiling tenderness for children, suitable to their ways and games and undoubtedly also a picture of a pious Brotherhood family. God gives children to parents " not only for delight and pleasure, but also for the work there is with them."

Immediately afterwards Komenský also composed another helpful book for children, the *Orbis pictus*, or the World in Pictures. This illustrated work was to serve two purposes. It was to be a practical handbook for those who were to turn children's attention from words to things and it also had to amuse children.

" We can neither act nor speak wisely unless we first understand well everything that is to be done or spoken about. And there is nothing in the intellect that has not been first in the sense. If we train our senses carefully so that they understand correctly the difference in things, we shall lay the foundations of all wisdom, all eloquence and all the prudent actions of life. But as this is generally neglected and the subjects which children have to learn are delivered to them incorrectly or without being thoroughly understood, then it happens that the instruction and learning can progress only very slowly and with poor results.

" It is the instruction itself which needs reforming, *better methods*. Not the memory alone should be trained. The children's souls contain seeds implanted there by nature, and the teacher should help these to germinate. Knowledge is to be imparted in a way that will lead the pupils to spontaneity. The true teacher is in the pupil himself. The birch rod has no place in the school ; the pupils should be punished only for offences against morality, not for playfulness or restlessness. The teacher should be kind and fatherly, distribute both praise and reward and, when fatigue sets in, be ready to show the children something to refresh their mind. The school should be cheery and not evade giving information about anything one may see at home or in the town every day.

" The school buildings should be light, airy, cosy and provided with paintings, maps, models and emblems with maxims. It is well to amuse the children with stories and allow them to dispute and struggle and play, this being good for their health. One of the important accessories of a pleasant school is to cultivate the majority of the principal mechanical arts, if for no other reason than for this : that nothing should take place in human life which could not be at least partly understood, or that the natural inclination would easier show itself."

It was Komenský who introduced in the schools the intuitive method of instruction.

It was Komenský who first claimed that the school existed not only to teach but to educate as well.

It was Komenský who demanded a democratic school, the same for the rich and the poor, for boys and for girls.

It was Komenský who presented his contemporaries with a clear plan of how to arrange schools according to the age and need of the children. Hence (1) a maternal school in every house ; (2) a common national school in every village, town and city ; (3) a Latin school (grammar school, gymnasium) in every county town ; and (4) a university (academy) in every country, this last to be supplemented by the travels of the students in foreign countries.

It was Komenský who established the maternal schools (Kindergarten) for children of the tenderest age. He also discovered the new science which made its aim the studying of the child, therefore not only of him who teaches but also of him who is being taught.

It was Komenský who prescribed that all instruction is to begin in the mother tongue. The foreign languages are to be taught later.

The sum total of all his principles is : " The true school is that where human wit is brightened by a true knowledge of all things ; where the characters and customs are arranged in noble harmony ; where the heart becomes firmly rooted in God and the tongue is variously shaped to pleasant eloquence. . . . All this should be taught in the schools, all, I say, without exception, because they desire to be called the *workshop of humanity*, which they also should be " (Didactica).

For these principles the history of pedagogy assigns to Komenský the foremost place among all school-reformers. Komenský certainly raised education to a science, by discovering the most important laws of all instruction, none of which can be ignored ; laws which are still valid, in force and beneficial.

The prominent thinkers of all times tried to create from human knowledge a system of thought and then to give this thought a certain course and rules. This is the work of philosophers. It is said, briefly, that philosophy makes for a uniform view of the world. Komenský was a philosopher and was much concerned to obtain such a view for himself. But he was not, in philosophy, a discoverer to the same extent as in pedagogy. As an educator he left behind him a broad ray of light which shone through several centuries. Yet even in philosophy Komenský occupies a high rank.

By the mere fact alone that in the conflict of several different philosophical systems he joined the one which stood for progress—the system of the English pioneer Lord Verulam, and of the French philosopher Descartes —is he deserving of that high rank. The new philosophy was born of the observation of nature, which was to form the basis for knowledge of the world. This watchword signified a rupture with the Bible as the all-governing code for human thought and research. Descartes was a great doubter. He taught that we know nothing for certain, that there is no absoluteness in knowledge and what is certain is only that man thinks, therefore that intellectual activity in a man is merely a condition of our attaining the knowledge of things external, behind which stands God as the originator of the world. The stand taken by the Catholic Church to this new philosophy was hostile from the beginning.

Komenský sought satisfaction for himself in this philosophy in such a way that he accepted it only in part and tried to reconcile the Bible with nature. This agrees fully with his theological principles. When the axiom was accepted that philosophy ought to be *pansophy*, or universal knowledge, and that it should give a perfect explanation of all that man knows, Komenský declared that true Christianity and pansophy were identical. He wanted to reconcile *nature* (the modern scientific spirit) with *Christianity* (founded on the Bible), so that there should be no conflict between them. Komenský understood that humanity resembles a man steadily advancing by degrees, and it was therefore clear to him that the new era must overtake the older era.   This faith of Komenský's in progress should be sufficient to make us moderns respect his genius.

Komenský's idea of a reconciliation of Christianity with philosophy is a manifestation of the spirit pervading the Bohemian Brotherhood, the manifestation of a desire in the topsy-turvy conditions of that period to unite all humanity in love, to make all mankind accept a harmonious view of the world, and to bring all this about by means of the Reformation and Protestantism.   Harmony of the man, of his reason and heart, theoretical and practical harmony in the world was the goal of his labours.   He, therefore, never hesitated to draw from the most rational thinkers, such as Bacon and Descartes, despite the fact that they were rejected by the old world and even pilloried in the Roman Index.   *Pansophy on a Christian basis* is the sense of Komenský's philosophy " so that, by the three principles of recognition : the senses, reason, and faith, unity in the knowledge of God, nature and art may be reached (Kádner)."   This pansophy was a kind of great encyclopædia, which would contain all human knowledge arranged harmoniously in one whole.

In pansophy Komenský took the liveliest interest. His pedagogical, as well as his theological, labours he considered mere preparation for pansophy, which was to have been his principal life's work.   Owing to the restless life he spent as an exile and his compulsory digressions to educational work, Komenský did not succeed in elaborating this pansophical system.   But even his preparations for a work comprising all human knowledge attracted the attention of the learned world. When his English friend Hartlib published (without Komenský's knowledge) in 1639 in London a pre-

liminary sketch of the *Pansofia prodromus*, which he
had received from Komenský, the eyes of the scientists
were at once directed to the Brotherhood philosopher.
Prominent men of all countries urged Komenský to go
on with so precious a work once begun. And the
English Parliament invited him to London to work at
it in England. Even America called on him to
assume the direction of Harvard University. Komenský went to England, where he published, in 1642, his
treatise *Via Lucis* (The Path of Light), in which he
explained his programme of the pansophy as follows :
it will do away with ignorance ; it will prevent war
(by a body of savants elected for that purpose in each
country) ; it will bring prosperity to the world ; it will
create new works and unite all thinking men by means
of a new language common to all, which will be invented to replace Latin. But he was able to publish,
in 1666 at Amsterdam, only the first two books, as
what he had previously prepared had been burnt at
Lešno.

Thus we have in Komenský theologian, pedagogue,
philosopher. However, this is not all that Komenský
was and still is to the Czech nation. To us he is,
besides, a great Bohemian Brotherhood patriot and a
politician. His *Didactic* he dedicated to the " *Czech
nation* and to all holding pre-eminence and rule there,
to the authorities and nobility, to the clergy and Church
administrators, to the town councillors, rectors of
schools, parents, etc.," in order that they may all work
for the restoration of their country. The restoration
of the country was to be accomplished by the education
of new and better generations than were those who
lived to see the year 1620. " Now since the Czechs
were driven into desolation, anyone who can give

advice, who can think of some remedy, or can obtain, by sighing, wailing and crying, from God anything that would benefit the growing youth in some way, such a one should not keep silence but should advise, think and entreat." " Let nobody say, Why should we commence such an unusual thing ? Let the French, the English and the Germans begin. Then we shall see how they will succeed. Let us not be, I beg, let us not be so lazy as to look always what others do and to crawl far behind them. They should sometimes see us ahead of them."

It was England to which Komenský's political hopes went out, for the " Winter King," Frederick, was son-in-law of the English King. At that time in England, Komenský unfolded in his work *Via Lucis* the idea which kindles our hearts even now. He turned back to the slightly altered idea, first pronounced by our Hussite King, i.e. that a body of the world's savants be formed into a tribunal, to which the nations should appeal in their international disputes, especially those to whom injustice was done. As England, where a civil war was then raging, could not help, Komenský looked to Sweden, where many Bohemian officers and soldiers had entered military service. He, therefore, took up again the difficult didactical work which he had previously put aside and devoted to it, from 1639, six years of his life. Trusting in the favour of the powerful Lord Chancellor of Sweden, with whom he had often personally discussed his plans, and also in that of the young Queen Christina, who knew him personally, he addressed to the Chancellor that plaintive letter of October 11th 1648—an epistle from each word of which tears seem to fall. After the disappointment of the Treaty of Westphalia

there remained perhaps only one hope in that respect
—the family of the Princes of Rakoczy.   So he gladly
accepted, when Henry II Rakoczy called him, in
1650, to Saryš Potok in Hungary, to organize the
Hungarian schools.   The younger brother of the
reigning prince, Sigmund, was the son-in-law of the
" Winter King " and, like his mother, was a great
admirer of Komenský.   For this Sigmund, Komenský
wrote the *Secret Speech of Nathan to David* (Sermo
secretus Nathanis in Davidom), in which the Prophet
Nathan charges Sigmund with the task of liberating
the downcast and oppressed Protestant churches—the
task of destroying Babylon—the Habsburg Empire.
Unfortunately, this prince soon died, in 1652.   For
George (Rakoczy) II, Komenský wrote a number of
sagacious political essays under the title of *A Nation's
Happiness* (Gentis felicitas).   The Court of Vienna
was already at that time apprised of Komenský's
propaganda.

   After the Treaty of Westphalia our nation was
plunged into darkness.   From that moment there was
nothing left but hopelessness and despair.   Komenský
alone did not despair, hoping that the resurrection of a
people, who were the first to suffer for Christ and the
Gospel, was only deferred.   This hope was expressed
by Komenský when, in 1650, he published at Lešno
the *Testament of a Dying Mother of the Brotherhood*, in
which, expecting to die soon, he bade farewell to his
nation and country.   In the years of the late war the
Bohemians piously recited to themselves Komenský's
prophecy from the Testament : " I also trust to God,
that after the tempest of wrath, that was brought upon
our heads by our sins, the rule of thy affairs will return
to thee, O thou people of Bohemia. . . . Live, thou

nation consecrated to God ; die not. May thy men
be without numbers. Bless, O Lord, its gallantry
and upon the toil of its hands look with favour. Break
the loins of its foes and those who hate it, so they rise
no more. . . ."

There were many who reproached Komenský that
a man so acute and enlightened as he should temporarily succumb to prophecies and superstitions fore-
telling of the future ; that he could take stock in the
then notorious visions of the German tanner Christo-
phes Kotter in Silesia, of the noble Polish girl Christina
Poniatovski, and finally of the companion of his youth,
the Brotherhood priest, Nicholas Drábek, a man of
disreputable character. But, after all, could anybody
wonder that a soul tormented with endless disappointment, and wandering hopelessly through the world for
forty long years, should direct its gaze to every will-o'-
the-wisp, taking it for a hint ? Could anybody judge
harshly a man believing in the Scriptures, from which
he drew the conviction that God sends to nations not
prophets alone but also special signs of His presence,
which then inspire both men and women to say things
out of the ordinary, " above the way of men " ?

Komenský's significance lies elsewhere. His greatness is already expressed in history by the fact that he
remained long misunderstood, because his religious,
educational and philosophical doctrines were, in that
era, " above the ways of men." There was a time
when, in Germany especially, he was grossly calum-
niated and underrated. But it was in this very country
again that the fullest satisfaction was accorded him by
the philosophers Leibnitz and Herder. Leibnitz
celebrated Komenský in a poem, and Herder, who
found in him " the dignity of an apostolic teacher,"

enrolled him among the pioneers of humanity.   Brock-
haus' Encyclopædia of the beginning of the nineteenth
century calls him " a benefactor of mankind."

His own nation was the last to appreciate him.
Even as late as 1892 the Catholic clergy, led by Bishop
Brynych and the Jesuit Svoboda, raised an outcry
against the celebrations in his honour, because, they
claimed, he was a married priest and an enemy of the
Habsburgs.   The Vienna government, of course,
gave in to the clerics readily enough, and the Minister
of Education, Gautsch, forbade the Komenský celebrations to be held in the schools.

Komenský was a prophet.   He could not, however,
like the ancient prophets and soothsayers, gather a
circle of disciples around him, for he was alone, a
wanderer over the world, and abandoned in the desolation of foreign lands.   He felt the distress of his
nation both on and in himself, although he knew of
the Lichtenstein Dragonnades and the merciless and
brutal missionaries in his country by hearsay only.
And, feeling this distress, he was conscious of his
responsibility.   On reading Komenský we have the
impression that a prophet is speaking to us from a
high mountain, where the weight of space and time is
not felt, and as if he were sending from there over the
past ages his prophecies to us of the future, not to his
contemporaries and fellow-sufferers alone, of whom he
was, moreover, not at all sure whether they were still
ready to open their ears and heart to his words.

And he was, indeed, a Bohemian, a Bohemian
Brotherhood prophet.

" To us Komenský must be more than he has
hitherto been.   We can recognize in him not only the
philosophy of the Bohemian Brotherhood, but the

philosophy of the Bohemian people, and of Bohemian history as well. In him we see not only an upright Bohemian, than whom there can be no better, but also a Bohemian working for the whole of mankind ; he writes in Bohemian, he writes in Latin—for the smaller circle of his people, for the large circle of the universe. . . . In Komenský we have the best example of real, sublime, ardent love for one's country, based on a general view of life, well considered and confirmed. The love for his own country and his own nation, however, does not prevent him working to uniting all men as brothers . . . (Masaryk)."

Silenced at last should be the groundless legend that the Bohemian Brotherhood led its followers to a life of non-resistance, to passivity and inactivity. In the whole of our history there has been no man more tireless, industrious and resolute. Of his writings only we now know almost 150. Instead of that the conviction should take root in us, that the love for our country does not demand our hating other nations ; for there are still many among us who cannot show their love for their nation otherwise than by abusing other nations. The virtues or defects of other nations should be extolled or castigated by their own people, but as for us, we should think and work and torment ourselves with joys or worries of our own.

Komenský's whole character—lovable, kind, noble —and his harmonious soul are expressed by his face. All the pictures of him preserved to us bear witness to that, most of all the portraits made by the Dutch painter Ovens, discovered as late as 1905, which hangs in the Imperial Museum of Amsterdam and which the Society *Dědictví Komenského* (Komenský's Inheritance) has circulated widely in our country. The

epitaph on his tomb at Naarden said justly of him
that—

" while studying truth, peace and wisdom,
    blessing his people and taking leave of the world,
    a mortal he ceased to be."

We have no physical relics of either of our two
greatest men. Huss' ashes were thrown into the Rhine
at Constance so the Bohemians could not carry them
away ; Komenský's ashes, mingled with others in the
damp Naarden tomb, were absorbed by moisture and
could not be transferred to Prague, although several
prominent men of the Bohemian Brotherhood Church
essayed the attempt lately.

In Komenský the Bohemian Reformation found its
culmination. With him everything had its roots in
care for the human soul. Therefore he was heroically
earnest, industrious to exhaustion, noble-minded and
unselfish to self-denial, and kind and loving even when
he had a reason to hate. A coarse word never passed
his lips. Morally, Komenský stood high above all
the Reformers of the sixteenth century, just as the
Brotherhood again exceeded by its morality all the
other religious societies. The mediæval age lay far
behind Komenský, for he stood for the principle of
truth and progress. This is why he is dear to the
Bohemians and precious to other nations.

While yet in its infancy, the Brotherhood accepted
some of the principles proclaimed by Peter Chelčický,
especially his aversion to theological learning, but
chiefly his opposition to all kinds of violence, which
to Chelčický was not only a Christian fighting with the
sword in general (not even religion should the Christian propagate by violence), but also assuming of

offices and of any kind of government.   Hence—not
to resist evil.   But during Brother Lukáš' time these
edges were ground off.   The Brothers accepted learning, the Brotherhood even becoming the centre of
the national culture.   Moreover, the Brethren also
accepted official positions, as they could not evade the
necessities of life, but, to give them credit, they learned
to manifest their Christianity in these offices as well as
in all other vocations.   They agreed with Calvin that
religious society should transform, in the spirit of the
Gospel, all conditions of life, thus also the political,
economic and social ones, so that everything serves
directly that which is desired by God, the extension
of the Kingdom of Heaven on earth.   The Bohemian
Brethren therefore gave heed to the laws, to economy,
to the country and municipal administration.   It was
exactly this efficiency which distinguished the Brotherhood from both the Calixtines and the Lutherans.
Luther subordinated the subjects to the authorities, bidding them also to pray for the latter.   In the
Brotherhood there were men who energetically took
either to the sword or to politics when religious liberty
was threatened.   That the rebellion against Ferdinand I, in 1554, ended with disaster was not Pluh's
fault; that the Protestants obtained from Rudolph II, in
1609, the Letter of Majesty, was the work of Budovec.
While the Lutherans in the Alpine region quickly suc-
cumbed to Ferdinand II's counter-reformation, the
Brethren in the Bohemian lands resisted his attack for
a long time.

It is not decisive for the Bohemian reformation that
it started with unclarified Calixtinism (already the
radical Táborites deserve our sympathies)—decisive
is, how far it went.   And the summit it reached in

the Brotherhood is also, politically, the most advanced grade of civic self-consciousness ever reached in the Middle Ages. After the extirpation of the Brotherhood, its spirit continued to live in other nations. For from the manner in which the Puritans carried through their glorious revolution in England and, a hundred years later, the American colonists declared for human rights, we can judge of the kind of people who were extirpated in the Bohemian countries following upon 1620. The true representative of the Brotherhood in the era subsequent to the White Mountain was then no other than Komenský.

VIII

Echo of the Bohemian Reformation in Other Countries

DID Hussitism and the Bohemian Brotherhood have any influence on the surrounding countries? Certainly, it could not be otherwise, and the influence was both for good and for evil.

Reports of the Bohemian heresy spread all over the Christian world with great rapidity. Even before the convocation of the Council of Constance Huss and his friends were known to the Popes and all other Church functionaries in France, Italy and England. And the news of Huss' death at the stake flew from Constance even quicker, for the whole Christian world was assembled there in the persons of its bishops, prelates and expounders of the Scriptures. From Constance also issued the watchword (uttered by Gerson) against the Bohemians to the effect that they should be wiped out by the sword.

The Church Council of Basle occupied itself with the Bohemian heresy almost to the exclusion of anything else. Pope Martin V gave only a tardy consent to its convocation, his and King Sigmund's intention having been to put the heretics to death first. In the meantime the Crusade of 1431, which was to be the last, ended in disgrace, and from that moment the question of peace or war in Europe was in the hands of the Hussite armies. The Crusaders fled from Domažlice on August 14th 1431, and already on the 15th of the following October the Bohemians were invited to Basle for peaceful negotiations. Unfortunately, the Council of Basle merely threw a halter over the necks of the Bohemians in the shape of the Compacts, and did not even keep its promise to send to all countries open letters which were to clear the Bohemians of the stigma of heresy laid on them by both Church Councils and the Pope.

To a still greater extent did the knowledge of Bohemian heresy spread over Europe through the direct contact with the Bohemians of the thousands of foreigners, who allowed themselves to be hired in the sign of the Cross to go and massacre the Bohemians, and were rewarded for this by absolution from all their sins and by good pay. The Crusaders were chiefly of German nationality, but there were also Hungarians, Italians, Frenchmen, Englishmen, Dutchmen, etc. Once the bloodthirsty Pope Martin gave to the crusading armies the English Cardinal Beaufort of Winchester for a leader, then again the Italian Cardinal Cesarini, not to mention the lesser bishops and German princes. The Crusaders returned, as far as they did return, to their countries, and in justifying their defeat, spread superstitious tales about the Bohemians, describing them as devils or as in league with the devil. In the subsequent Crusades—against the Hussite King George—the Bohemians were painted in the same way.

Twice did the Hussite armies carry the terror of their name into the neighbouring countries. The

Germans met the Bohemian heretics face to face when the latter, under Prokop the Great, threatened both the German South and North, when the Táborite warriors watered their horses in the Danube or bathed them in the Baltic. Even Hamburg trembled before them and hurriedly repaired its fortifications. In the time of the Hussite King, when peace reigned at home, the Táborite captains held sway over both Slovakia and Croatia, extending the glory of the strategic art of the Bohemians still further.

This was all the evil there was in the relations of the Bohemians with their neighbours.

Their influence, however, was also fruitful. And it could not be otherwise. For it had been observed already, during the European Crusades to Palestine and those against the heathen Prussians, that enemies, while fighting each other with the sword, adopt from each other many customs as well as ideas and even mental disposition. And this is exactly what happened in the case of the Hussites—their mentality did not remain without influence either. Enough is left on record for us to know now that in the countries bordering on Bohemia there had been even during the wars many who did not regard the Bohemians as enemies, but whose souls were even filled with Hussite heresy.

In Poland Hussitism took deep root. The Poles had an opportunity of getting to know the Bohemians intimately. The Hussite Bohemians wished to have a member of the Jagellon family for their king and thus the religious movement became involved with political ideas. At no later time did the Slavonic relationship of the Bohemians with the Poles become as close as in the days of Žižka and George of Poděbrad. It began at Grünwald. The Polish people had already heard Jerome and understood the later Bohemian preachers entirely, and thus Hussitism gained many adherents among the lower clergy, and especially so in the knightly ranks. Then the idea grew in the minds of the nobility of amalgamating Bohemia with Poland into one State. Following this a strong Hussite party was formed in Poland. The Polish historian, M. Bobrzynski, says that the bosom of the Polish nation enclosed anti-Roman elements waiting only for a watchword to do in Poland what was being done in Bohemia. The endangered hierarchy, headed by the Cracow bishop, Zbyněk Olešnický, who dominated the royal court, then exerted its whole strength. Tumults against the Catholic hierarchy broke out into a danger-ous flame ; in 1438 and 1439 we find two opposing confederations, but Zbyněk Olešnický defeated the Bohemian-Hussitic party in a bloody battle at Grotník and followed it up by taking the castles of the Hussite nobles, confiscating their property and burning the Hussite priests at the stake.

But what the German Crusaders expected perhaps least of all, actually happened ; Hussitism began to set the minds of numerous German priests afire. In Germany too, in many places the smoke of the faggot was seen. Among the first German priests to be accused of Hussitic heresy was the Erfurt theologian, Johann Wesel ; after him the " agrarian saint," Böhm, was dragged before the tribunal of the Inquisition. In Worms Johann Drähndorf was burnt at the stake in 1425, being convicted of eighteen Táborite " errors " ; at Speyer, in 1426, his friend, Peter Turnov, met with the same fate. None of them retracted. The preacher, Friedrich Reiser, a supposed

Waldensian, suffered in 1458, but he was convicted
of having communicated with Magister English and
of having lived at Tábor, where he was consecrated a
priest by Mikuláš Pelhřimovský ; also of having
accompanied the Bohemian envoys to Basle, etc.
Hussite, too, was a German from the North, Matthew
Hagen, who propagated Hussitism in Brandenburg
and was burnt in 1458. Another more famous
follower of Hussitism in the North, was Nicholas
Rutze, whom fate allowed to die a natural death, probably in 1508. He translated the following works of
Huss : *The Threefold Chord, Explanation of Faith, The
Ten Commandments,* and *Lord's Prayer,* although being
himself rather of the Waldensian confession. His
efforts were considered as Hussite propaganda in the
Low Countries.

We know, of course, that Hussites were burnt at
the stake in Holland too. French peasants, again, in
some districts, attracted by the Táborite ideas, refused
to obey the authorities. A letter of the Maid of
Orleans, written in Latin, has also been preserved to
us. A forgery, perhaps, but even then it is interesting
to learn that she had heard of the Hussites, and that
she threatened to march to Bohemia and extirpate the
whole sinful race as soon as she had finished with the
English.

But that a Hussite met death at the stake also in distant Scotland, is surprising. Unfortunately, not even
the most competent Church historians can tell us anything more definite than that Paul Kravař came to
Scotland from Bohemia and that he was a good physician but a still better Hussite. The movement
against the Church existed in the fifteenth century in
Scotland as in all other countries, and the first victim

there was the Wyclifite John Resby, an Englishman, who was burnt in 1408 ; but at the second stake fire there perished the Bohemian, Paul Kravař. He had a circle of followers, became suspected of having been purposely sent by the Hussites to Scotland, was arrested and arraigned before Inquisitor Lindorese, who had already sent Resby to the stake. Kravař defended himself by the Scriptures and by, it is alleged, " incontrovertible " proofs. Yet, in spite of all that, he was burnt, on July 23rd 1433, in the public square at St. Andrew's. To prevent him from addressing the people from the stake, his mouth was gagged with a pear made of metal.

The Japanese professor, Aan A. Ozolin, in his pamphlet *The oldest European Nation, Facts about Latvia* (1920), writes : " The small communities of Moravian Brethren, inspired by the doctrines of John Amos Komenský and Count Zinzendorf, taught the Latvians that all men are equal before God and men. In the region of the influential Courland nobility this doctrine was considered, especially by a part of the clergy, as politically revolutionary and therefore inconvenient. As a consequence its representatives were, in the nineteenth century, sent to Siberia. The movement, however, greatly inspired Latvian literature with its ideas."

When the fifteenth century was nearing its end, the Bohemian nation lived separately from all its neighbours, universally hated, exhausted by its second defensive wars against Rome, impoverished economically, and politically led by its two weak Polish Kings towards utter insignificance. It was the German historian, Franz von Bezold, who wrote the following about us : " It is sometimes the tragic fate of nations

that they conduct terrible wars for the benefit of the
whole of humanity, but in doing so sacrifice the flower
of their manhood and their whole strength. Not for
the liberation and greatness of his people did the Hussite warrior gain victory after victory, but for the
liberation and awakening of his hated antagonist, the
Germans in the first place (Zur Geschichte des Hussi-
tenthums)." In what dislike the Bohemians then
were with all their neighbours we see in Luther's case.
How scared was he when his opponent Eck, accepting
Luther's challenge to a public disputation, called out
to him : " Thou art a heretic and a Bohemian ! "
Our dear Luther knew nothing better to say in his
haste to clear himself of such a charge, than to declare
in his next sermon that he who would impute Bohemian heresy to him, lied. But it is almost touching
to observe how Luther softened, step by step, after
becoming acquainted with Huss' doctrines, until, at
the beginning of 1520, he wrote to Spalatini : " Thus
far I have, although unconsciously, proclaimed all
that Huss preached and maintained ; John Staupitz
did, unconsciously, maintain the same—in a word, we
are all Hussites, without having known it ; Paul and
Augustin themselves are Hussites—in the full sense
of the word ! Behold the horrible misery which came
over us because we did not accept the Bohemian
doctor for our leader . . . ! " And what was at first
done unconsciously, was soon done in all consciousness ; that is, Luther set himself to learn of Huss and
his teaching.

When, some time later, Luther came to know
the Bohemian Brotherhood, he gave its inner life
the warmest of recommendations. " Although the
Brothers do not excel us in purity of their doctrines

. . . yet by the orderly Church discipline which they make use of and through which they administer their congregations happily, they are far above us. . . ."

The influence of the Brotherhood on the foreign countries did not amount to much at first. For it resembled, to the end of the fifteenth century, according to Blahoslav, a child that is just beginning to talk. Not until Luther learned of it, did other Germans, too, become interested. The greatest attention to it was called by Ferdinand I, with whose Machiavellian policy it began to interfere. This monarch tried to consolidate the Calixtines with the Catholics, while the Brothers, noticing the invigorating effect of Lutheranism on the Calixtines, drew them away from Rome. The King, however, contrived to incite both the Calixtines and Catholics against the Brethren and utilized the mutual hostility of the two parties to renew, after the failure of the rebellion in 1547, the Breslau mandate against the Picards. By this act he sent the Brotherhood into exile. But wherever the Brethren settled there they also implanted their doctrines. Thus arose in Poland an important branch of the Brotherhood, particularly in Posen. It found a great zealot in the person of Jacob of Ostrorog, a magnate of Poland. From there the Bohemian ministers carried their doctrine into the very interior of Russia, and when it seemed that the Czar Ivan the Terrible was inclining to Protestantism, the Bohemian brother John Rokyta appeared at his court and held a religious disputation with him, in May 1570.

At the end of the sixteenth century we see Bohemian politics in the hands of the Brotherhood nobility. The Letter of Majesty of 1609 was the work of the knight Budovec. According to Denis the Bohemian, heretics were at that period exactly what they had been in the beginning : the defenders of the rights of the conscience, whose cause is the cause of civilization and progress.

The Polish noble Lasicki, when describing his arrival in 1571 at the Brotherhood town of Mladá Boleslav, exclaims : " O immortal God, What joy was then kindled in my heart ! Verily, it seemed to me, when I observed and inquired about everything, that I was in the church of Ephesus or Thessalonica or some other apostolic church ; here I saw with my own eyes and heard with my own ears such things as we read in apostolic letters and in the letters of Ignatius and in Justin's and Tertullian's Apologies. . . . Surely neither the Bohemian nor the Moravian country know what kind of inhabitants they have, or they would treat them with more respect and love them better than they do. . . ."

Germany also had many admirers of the Brotherhood. The famous Greek scholar and friend of reformers, Joachim Camerarius (1500–1574), who lectured successively at Nuremberg, Tubingen and Leipsic, wrote a laudatory historical work on the Brothers (with brief Passion essays by Huss and Jerome). As it would take too long to describe the influence of Hussitism and the Brotherhood in Germany, therefore I would refer the reader to the work of Prof. Ernest Kraus, *Hussitism in Literature in its First Two Centuries.*

The light of the Brotherhood shone abroad where it was expiring in exile, after 1620, and it was shining even after it expired, not unlike those distant stars which, although already extinct, continue to throw their light for thousands of years on the terrestrial

globe. For to what place did the Bohemian exiles
not turn, where is it that we cannot find traces of them ?
They lived in distress in all Germany, taught in
Poland, served in the Swedish army, hid in France and
England, sought and found refuge in Holland. And
our exiles were the flower of their nation. Members
of the nobility or the middle classes, they were largely
people of the highest intelligence, among them artists
(like Hollar) and writers (such as Komenský, Stránský,
Skála, etc.) ; also people of substance, and in religion
alive and steadfast. Can anybody imagine that they
could remain without religious and cultural influence
on their surroundings ? Komenský, Stránský, Bor-
bonius, the Žerotins. . . . Yes, we even find the
Bohemian exiles on the other shore of the Atlantic
ocean. The preacher Telčík stayed in North America
only temporarily. More permanent was the sojourn
of two former citizens of Prague, Augustin Heřman,
who appeared in New York in 1633, and, with him,
Frederick Filip. Both came there from Holland and
at once attracted attention. Heřman was a surveyor,
Filip a merchant. Both made large fortunes, besides
holding important offices in their new country. Then
there were Zaborovskýs in America, and one of the
Páca family who, in 1776, signed the Declaration of
Independence for the State of Maryland, was believed
to be of Bohemian descent.

About the religious activities of these individuals
we know but little (only in the Heřman family a liking
for the Labadist sect is said to have manifested itself).
But to make up for that the efforts of the Restored
Brotherhood met with considerable success and were
greatly appreciated. The Restored Brotherhood were
the Moravian Brethren of German nationality from

around Fulnek who, after escaping from Moravia, founded, in 1722, with the permission of Count Zinzendorf, a new settlement and church community on his domain of Herrnhut. The doctrines of this society have a tinge of Pietism, but the church discipline remained the same. In America it was simply called " the Moravians." The first settlement there was founded, by emigrants from Herrnhut, in Georgia, in 1735, the Bohemian, Anthony Seifert, being its first preacher. Its prayer-house was consecrated by the bishop of Herrnhut, David Nitschman, in the presence of the founder of the Methodist church, John Wesley. The Herrnhuters became missionaries, converting both Indians and negroes. In course of time the settlement of Bethlehem became the headquarters of their activity. Bohemian relics and books still exist there ; sermons dealing with Huss and Komenský were, and probably still are, preached there, and there also is an interesting cemetery, where an Indian lies beside a white man—the first example of the democracy of which the Americans are so proud.

Another Herrnhuter, Matthew Stach, a Moravian by birth, became an apostle to the Eskimos in Greenland and laboured among them from 1733 to 1772. Thomas Čapek, who collected the *Memorials of the old Bohemian Immigrants to America* in a book published in 1907, says of these old Moravians : " They often were the first to bring light into the sheer darkness of ignorance among uncultured and barbarous nations, they wrested the murderous club from the hand of the savage, and taught him to forgive. It was not, of course, easy work."

When was it, then, that Hussitism and the Brotherhood perished in their own country ? It was when the remnants of the Hussites and Brethren, although still remembering the past of the old churches and considering themselves heirs of both Huss and Komenský, were compelled to accept the confessions then existing in Germany : the Helvetian and Augsburg. Yet the spirit did not disappear even if the name did. The Gospel, though only tolerated, permitted to rise, in its spirit, a Kollár, a Šafařík and a Palacký, who built for the awakened nation in the nineteenth century the foundation pillars of the national programme.

The restored Brotherhood left in Germany remarkable traces in the character of eminent men.　Immediately affected by Herrnhut were Lessing in Saxony, Herder in Riga, Kant in Koenigsberg and Goethe in Frankfurt.　All this was a continuation of the influence exerted by Komenský on Leibnitz.　In the " land of their fathers " the Brotherhood founded several congregations in the second half of the nineteenth century.

After the World War the liberated nation began to settle accounts with both Vienna and Rome.　On the ruins of old Austria there was established the promising Czecho-Slovak Republic, a new State.　In the meantime, the religious movement after the revolution bore this fruit : Both Bohemian confessions, conceded to the Protestants in 1781, were united into one Brotherhood Church, which represents over 250,000 members.　But a million Catholics left Rome to found a new Czecho-Slovak Church, and they have advanced, in their doctrines and organization, much farther beyond the boundary of reforms than the ideal of the reformed Roman Church set up by Havlíček in his *Epistles of Kutná Hora.*

EPILOGUE

The Nineteenth and Twentieth Centuries

THE person of Huss became a rock on which the Bohemian nation split into two camps. The nation, although remaining homogeneous lingually, became disunited religiously—Hussite and Catholic. Numerically these two Bohemian peoples have changed. From the time of the Hussite wars to the battle of the White Mountain (1620) the number of the adherents of the Chalice grew to such an extent that at the beginning of the seventeenth century there were in the Bohemian countries 90 per cent. Protestants (of this about 10 per cent. Bohemian Brothers) and barely 10 per cent. Catholics. A Moravian topographer, a Catholic, when working on the Church topography of Moravia in 1600, could not find even ten Catholic parishes there at that time. After the battle of the White Mountain a retrograde movement took place. The Proscription, the Thirty Years' War and a pestilence all caused the population of the Bohemian crown-lands, Bohemia, Moravia and Silesia, to sink to scarcely half its previous number. In the middle of the seventeenth century, the Kingdom of Bohemia had about 800,000 ; Moravia, with the Troppau and Teschen districts, barely 500,000 inhabitants, and this whole mass was so thoroughly

Catholic that when the Emperor Joseph II issued his famous Patent concerning the toleration of Protestants in the Habsburg Empire, no more than 70,000 clandestine Protestants—that camp of the Hussites —made their appearance.   But even so the intellectual significance of this " hidden seed " (Komenský's words) was, culturally, of more importance in the revival period than the whole mass of the Catholicized people.

Since the time of Huss and Žižka the Bohemian nation also has a twofold history, each part of which mutually excludes the other.   Where it is the task of an unbiased historian to tell his people in what manner the development of the nation has progressed from the time of the migration to our days—which means showing him the spirit of its different dynasties and governments, the pictures of its life and people's morals, the extension of its territory by conquest, the social changes and economic spirit—there the author can more easily arrive at the leading national ideal and the common principles of the civic wisdom for the instruction of later generations, for then nothing tempts him to describe events falsely.   But where history lives in the shadow of religious conviction, there the temptation is irresistible.   However, to such a temptation the temporal historians are rarely exposed ; the less so the more indifferent they are religiously.   On the other hand, the histories of the Bohemian nation, contemplated in a Catholic spirit and especially when written by Catholic priests, are usually clouded by partisan breath so as to be divided by a deep chasm from reality and truth.   Unfortunately, the first Bohemian history of the era of Huss and King George was written by Aeneas Sylvius, the later Pope

Pius II. This history became, from the fifteenth century, the favourite text-book of Europe as it contained almost as many strange, adventurous and even incredible matters that it could easily compete with Mandeville's Travels and with the popular romances of that period.

A hundred years after him a Calixtine convert, the priest Václav Hájek of Libočan, who became a favourite of the Catholic hierarchy, popularized Aeneas Sylvius on a broad scale, and by the falsities, inventions and infamies which he added during the reign of the first Habsburg to occupy the Bohemian throne, he has undoubtedly surpassed all historians of his faith in the Old and the New World. At the end of the seventeenth century the Jesuit Bohuslav Balbín, who wrote in Latin, and Fr. Beckovský, of the Order of the Knights of the Cross, who wrote in Bohemian, became enamoured of Bohemian history. The whole nineteenth century was not long enough for our historians —Palacký, Tomek, Gindely, Goll, Rezek, etc.—to purge our history of all the fables, lies and distortions which were heaped by these Roman Catholic historians upon our national past.

Of course, the Catholic party always wrote spitefully about Huss and Žižka. Huss was to the Catholic priests an object of ridicule while he lived, and he preached his sermons and served Mass, it was said, in ordinary barns. Žižka, again, was to them an executioner, a great criminal and miserable traitor.

Aeneas Sylvius spread his fables and calumnies about Huss and Žižka over the whole known world. For the Bohemian nation his *Historia Bohemica* was a catastrophe of the first order, as it was written in elegant Latin, with humanitarian wit, and made Bohemian history read like a popular novel. He wrote about the Bohemians in the interest of the Papacy, for the tiara of which he was then already stretching out his hand. Sylvius was the originator of the ugly fable that the dying Žižka ordered his soldiers to make a drum of his skin, with which to terrify his enemies. All the later historians repeated this monstrosity; it was known to Voltaire and believed by the Prussian King Frederick II. Native historians of the Hussitic Period we lack almost entirely. The people of erudition were then so preoccupied with the "wrath of the day" and the various confessions and dogmatic disputes, that they scarcely wrote anything for their descendants.

But the aftermath of the battle of the White Mountain was yet to come. In that period the canons, Jesuits and monks, Dubravius, Pešina, Kořínek, Balbín, Beckovský and some lesser ones, had everything to say. Listen to Balbín. To him the Hussite and Brotherhood era was a time of shame, notwithstanding that Bohemia had both literary and political glory from it in the time of Charles IV and the Ferdinands. The name of Huss Balbín did not pronounce at all. He merely classed him, anonymously, with the "venomous heretics."

Hear what Kořínek has to say of Žižka. He put his views into the mouth of a fancied preacher of the year 1419: "the Táborites are a mob of savages, an untamed rabble, a band of godless slaves, a gang of sacrilegious thieves, a cohort of ravishers of noble nations and pure virgins, a regiment of plunderers of sacred objects, an army of Bohemian highwaymen. Their leader is a certain John Žižka of Trocnov, a haughty and insolent little squire who, before he got

HUSS AT THE STAKE.

[To face p. 208

rich by robbing the churches, was the Lord of Poor-town and Havenought Boroughs, strutted about in boots with spurs, but his steed was stuck in a rail fence ; a very scamp. He sees with only one eye, because the other one they knocked out in a skirmish (ah ! would they had knocked out his brains too !) ; is popular with the fickle people because he made the town of Prague put on its armour against King Václav ; an ugly monster, whom the finger of God will some-where wipe out yet ! "

Žižka's tomb at Čáslav, whither his body was in course of time transferred from Hradec Králové, was, after the battle of White Mountain, plundered and destroyed. According to some writers the body of Žižka was buried under the gallows. This seems to have been only a pious wish, as in our time a walled-in skull has been found in Čáslav church, to which all the circumstances point as having belonged to Žižka.

In such spirit was Bohemian history placed before the Bohemian nation, on its native soil, all through the era of the Counter-Reformation. The Bohemian exiles could at least read Skála, Stránský and Komen-ský, while at home, in the land of their fathers, a dense darkness spread over the whole country. Its last phase was portrayed to the nation by Jirásek in his *Temno* (darkness).

In the National Museum at Prague there may be seen a letter, considerably damaged, which was written by Huss against his calumniators in 1411. The Hussite writer, Sixtus of Ottersdorf, added to it, in 1546 : " This letter was written in his own hand by the divine John Huss of sacred and pious memory, the most steadfast martyr of our Lord Jesus Christ." But on the other side is written : " The superscription of this letter was written by a heretic Hussite ; this letter was found in the library of the archbishop by John Thomas Berghauer, an alumnus, in 1706, and was, for the memory of antiquity, put behind glass in 1711, so that all who will read it may curse the baseness of a heretic." This Berghauer later became a Canon and a famous biographer of " Saint " John of Nepomuk.

Behold these two dates : 1546 and 1706.

Our national awakening at the end of the eighteenth century at first resulted only in the enlightenment of individuals, but immediately afterwards national consciousness and sentiment flamed up, after a lapse of 150 dark years. The work of our " awakeners " resembled that of archæologists. The historians excavated from under the débris the rest of the Bohemian Hussites and the Brotherhood, the philologists excavated the old standard Czech language from decaying and hidden memorials, especially from the Králice Bible. There ensued a general direction of minds to the past, the period of which the Reformation came to its end. It is especially worthy of note that the new historians turned away from the Catholic historians Hájek and Balbín, accused them of falsehood and lying, and began independently to examine Huss and Žižka, the Brotherhood and Komenský. The leader and representative of this work of enlightenment was Dobrovský, of whom Ernest Denis did not hesitate to say that he, over Komenský's head, shook hands with Huss. Not that the awakeners wanted to be Hussites or Brethren themselves—but they desired to revive reverence for the men and the ideas by which the Hussites, like the Brethren, had succeeded in uplifting their nation.

Was it possible for this newly-awakened people to read Bohemian history without long-forgotten religious ideals being aroused in them ? Could anybody sit among pious people and not be himself captivated by their piety ? To me, at least, reading the lives of our reformers and martyrs, the perusal of their books and their reflections seems like religious reverie.

The treasures brought to the surface by the archæologists were at once seized upon by the poets, writers and journalists. Among the treasures the foremost were Huss, Žižka and Komenský, the whole Bohemian Reformation. But lest anybody be surprised that, even after the Toleration Patent, our intelligentsia failed to embrace the doctrines of Huss and the Bohemian Brethren *en masse*, he must know that the Patent (1781) did not permit the restoration of the old Bohemian Confessions, but simply ordered that the secret Protestants living in the country till then, must decide for either the Helvetian or Augsburg confession. There was another and more fatal reason. The enlightened circles, even among the Bohemians, saw in Joseph's ecclesiastical and anti-papal reforms the beginning of a new Reformation, perhaps the same which was centuries ago instituted from above by Henry VIII in England. " We are living in a new Reformation ! " exclaimed one of the " enlightened " zealots. Evidently this new Josephite reformation seemed to its contemporaries more penetrating and more in accord with the spirit of enlightenment than that of the Protestant churches. Therefore they waited. But Joseph II reigned only ten years, from 1780 to 1790.

A great disappointment was to come. The Emperor Francis I, making use of the scare spread by the

French revolution and the Napoleonic. conquests, terrified the free-thinking spirits to such an extent that in the reaction which followed all the embryos of the " enlightened " period were stifled, and that with the help of the encouraged hierarchy, the reactionary nobility and the narrow-minded, dependent bureaucracy. In this reaction also perished the insignificant religious movement.

It was only after the Great European War that our restored independence gave rise to a new religious movement. A Bohemian Brother, Masaryk, became President of the Republic. From October 1918 to the end of 1923 that " heavenly light," which came down upon Saul on the road from Jerusalem to Damascus ages ago, struck also more than a million of the Czechs living in Bohemia, Moravia and Silesia. They left the Roman Church and founded a new Czecho-Slovak Church. The restored Bohemian Brotherhood, which, in 1918, immediately after the revolution, rejected the foreign denominations and returned to the Church of Komenský, gained over 70,000 new members. But let no one think that the remaining six millions of Czechs are all orthodox Romans. They are, for the most part, though religiously indifferent, devoted worshippers of John Huss, the warrior Žižka, King George, and admirers of the Bohemian Brotherhood, which gave our nation men like Blahoslav and Komenský. This is something foreign visitors can never understand. They see that a Catholic Prague erected, on its most memorable square, a monument to Huss, and that monuments to Huss, Žižka and Komenský are scattered all over the country by the hundred. And the separation with Rome is not yet complete, although great numbers of former

Catholics remain, in the meantime, without confession. [1]

The sole exception is Slovakia, which was, for one thousand years, throttled by the Magyars and whose thousand years of history culminated in this modern era in cultural vacuity and political enslavement. The majority of the Slovak intelligentsia consists of Catholic priests. And because the Catholics there number more than two millions, the Protestants scarcely half a million, and because the dark, illiterate element left to us by the Magyar and Jesuit influence exceeds 30 per cent. of the whole, there is little hope that Bohemian Hussitism or the Brotherhood will soon strike root there. Hence the " Darkness " (see Jirásek *Temno*) inherited by the Czecho-Slovak Republic weakens us also politically, for the present, of course. Two cultures clash like two geological strata. However, the time cannot be far away when the newly-rising Slovak intelligentsia will comprehend that without the Bohemian Reformation there could be no Slovak History.

We are Czechs, we are Slavs, and we became cognizant during the last hundred years of the fact that our mission lies in these two directions. But we also desire to follow those Bohemian reformers who laid the foundations of our historical glory.

For, we ask ourselves with Macaulay, what constitutes the difference between the earth and the Heavens ? And, like him, we also answer : " Not the fertility of the soil, not the mildness of the climate, nor mines, nor harbours and rivers. All these things are, of course, precious, when used by human reason for the purpose for which they were destined. Yet human reason can do much without them, while they alone, without human reason, can do nothing. Nature destined Egypt and Sicily to be the gardens of this world. Gardens they once were. Is there anything on earth or in the air, that makes Scotland happier than Egypt, that makes Holland happier than Sicily? No, indeed. But the Scotchman made Scotland what it is, the Dutchman made Holland what it is. The English emigrants brought little wealth with them to the American wilderness, but they brought—their *spirit*."

We Bohemians have not a large State and numerically, too, we are a rather small nation. But there were still less of the Hussites and Brethren in the fourteenth century, and yet they contrived to give light to Europe. Such are our aspirations for the future.